LEO MADOW, M.D.

GUILT

*How to Recognize
and Cope with It*

JASON ARONSON INC.
NORTHVALE, NEW JERSEY, LONDON

Library of Congress Cataloging-in-Publication Data

Madow, Leo, 1915–
   Guilt: how to recognize and cope with it / by Leo Madow.
     p.   cm.
   Bibliography: p.
   Includes index.
   ISBN 0–87668–923–3
   1. Guilt–Psychological aspects.   2. Guilt–Psychological aspects–
Case studies.   I. Title.   BF575.G8M22 1988   152.4–dc19   88–3438
                                                CIP

Manufactured in the United States of America

Jason Aronson Inc. offers books and cassettes. For information and catalog write to Jason Aronson Inc. 230 Livingston Street, Northvale, N.J. 07647

Dedicated to Ma and to all mothers,
not in guilt but in love.

Contents

v

Introduction

All of us have such potential for enjoyment and pleasure that it is difficult to understand why something always seems to get in our way. We have bodies that can take in and digest food in a remarkable sequence of processes, drawing the nourishment from it, storing energy as needed, and eliminating the wastes. We can run 27-mile marathons and we can perform microsurgery. Our brain is more intricate than the best-developed computer. The human eye cannot be matched by the most sophisticated of electronic devices. We are able to perform the three Rs and to place a man on the moon. We are capable of careful reasoning and of awe-inspiring creativity. We may travel thousands of miles for the pleasure of seeing a Mona Lisa or spend months of work for the gratification of growing a rose.

Despite this remarkable physical and mental apparatus, we manage with this same finely tuned organism to torture ourselves with exquisite finesse, sometimes to an unbearable point. Often we cannot turn it off.

Somewhere in this protoplasmic composition, we have emotions. Some emotions consist of great and wonderful experiences, such as the feelings associated with falling in love and the pleasure of creation. Other emotions are negative and painful and may be counterproductive to the ultimate point of self-destruction.

One of the most painful of these emotions is guilt. How can we be reasonable and at times brilliant, yet in many ways manage to make our lives miserable through feelings of guilt?

A woman feels guilty if she doesn't call her mother every day. A man yells at his child for misbehaving and is tormented with guilt afterward. A young woman has sex on a first date, then

3

agonizes over it, certain she did wrong and will never hear from the man again. There are many people who feel guilty about masturbation and believe they have harmed themselves because of it. A 65-year-old woman who had a slight stroke is beset with guilt, feeling she has become an intolerable burden to her husband.

Guilt is a ubiquitous emotion. We all feel it in varying amounts and for different reasons. We experience some form of it almost every day of our lives. We generate guilt in ourselves, we stimulate it in others, and all too often we don't know where it comes from or how to relieve the pain and suffering it engenders.

One of the more disturbing features of guilt is the sense that one has no control over it. We are often aware that others would not feel the least bit guilty for having done the same thing we did. We wonder why we not only feel guilty about a certain act but also continue to torment ourselves long after the deed was done. Sometimes people are not even conscious of their guilt feelings and develop emotional disturbances. Indeed, most patients who see psychotherapists are struggling with problems of guilt, of which they are unaware but which may be producing emotional and physical symptoms. Guilt is like anger—there are times when we are aware of it and tormented by it because we don't know what to do with it. On the other hand, many times we feel guilt about something and do not recognize what we are feeling. Subsequently, this guilt may manifest itself in many ways, often producing symptoms such as depression or phobias.

How is it possible to feel guilty about something and not know it? We all have feelings we are afraid of. Sometimes when we are enraged enough, we may actually feel like harming someone. This frightens us. It is not too uncommon for parents to become so infuriated with their children that it scares them, believing that this means they do not love the children. They feel guilty about having such feelings and back away from them by denying them. We also feel guilty about some angers because they are forbidden (for example, it is wrong to hate your father) and thus the anger must be denied. Both the anger and guilt are repressed, and symptoms such as compulsions may appear, the person being completely unaware of the anger or the guilt. This is the most difficult type of guilt to deal with. How can one resolve guilt feelings when one does not even know he or she has them? One of the purposes of this book is to help recognize hidden guilt feelings and to learn to deal with these feelings so that they do no harm.

Is guilt really a prevalent emotion? The story of guilt goes back as far as human history. It is told that almost immediately after their creation, Adam and Eve ate the forbidden fruit. When they heard the sound of God walking in the forest, they hid from Him. They knew they had done wrong and felt guilty. Their punishment was so immediate and so frightening that people hearing this powerful story in their childhood develop a picture of a personal punitive God who observes everything they do and approves or disapproves. This process contributes to the formation of a conscience and its accompanying guilt feelings.

Sometimes the things about which we feel guilty change. The so-called sexual revolution has created new problems in guilt. The young man may no longer feel guilty about having sex with a woman. His guilt now stems from the feeling that he cannot satisfy her. Some women feel guilty if a man does not want to have sex with them, wondering if they did something wrong.

Guilt is not entirely a subject for tragedy. Comedians have developed entire routines on guilt, particularly guilt generated by mothers. One (Morty Gunty) declares his mother has the East Coast distributorship on guilt. She even has a toll-free 800 number should anyone feel too good and need a quick guilt fix.

Another classic story concerns the mother who calls her son or daughter and says, "Hello. This is your mother. Remember me?"

"Jewish guilt" is not the exclusive prerogative of Jewish mothers. As Gunty says:

All my non-Jewish friends have mothers who say the same kinds of things in different dialects. The truth is that all women go to the same Mothers' School. They get a special test. If they fail, they become aunts instead.

The tremendous power of guilt was demonstrated by a story reported from Israel. Mrs. Cohen was a spry woman in her seventies who entered her Jerusalem apartment and found a thief ransacking it in a nonchalant, professional manner.

She did not scream "Help!" or "Police!" but drew herself up to her full height of 4' 9", shook her fist at the man, and yelled, "I'll tell your mother!"

The thief panicked, dropped everything, and fled from the apartment.

The martyr complex is dependent for its effectiveness on its generation of guilt in the people involved. The comic strip "Momma" by Mel Lazarus describes Momma's unending series of ploys to control her children, including playing the martyr, often generating tremendous guilt in her family. Her children's reactions vary from compliance, sometimes overcompliance, to resentment, to outright resistance. The martyr generates guilt in the victim by passive suffering, which is actively reported to the receiving person with the implications that it is his or her fault and that it is up to that person to remove the suffering. Accepting the blame leads to guilt.

Psychiatrists are interested in helping patients deal with their *unrealistic guilt* feelings: the woman who is convinced that all her children's difficulties are derived from her poor mothering, the man who torments himself because he believes he drove his wife to an affair, the woman who feels it is her fault that she became pregnant or can't become pregnant, the Holocaust survivor who feels guilty because he "made it" and so many didn't. These are the people seen in therapists' offices seeking relief.

Joshua Liebman (1946) points out the dangers of excessive guilt:

> *The same marvelous faculty that guides us along the road to morality often acts as a sadistic slave-driver, a self-accusing fury, and a tireless jobber in guilt. The damage wrought by these aspects of conscience is incalculable. Much of our mental and physical illness, a whole list of fears, anxieties,*

and hatreds spring from the seeds of false conscience that
man has somehow contrived to sow during his life.

Huckleberry Finn says, "It don't make no difference whether
you do right or wrong, a person's conscience ain't got no sense and
just goes for him anyway. If I had a yaller dog that didn't know no
more than a person's conscience does, I would pison him."

Not all guilt feelings are harmful. Guilt and guilty fear have
played an important role in the survival of society. Without an
appropriate amount of guilt there would be no civilization. This
will be discussed when we consider the origins of a sense of guilt.

We should also keep in mind that some people's behavior
would be unacceptable, unpleasant, or even antisocial if they had
no feelings of guilt.

The purpose of this book is to investigate the origins of guilt;
how much, if any, is appropriate to a particular stituation; what
are the major issues about which we feel guilty; how may the guilt
manifest itself; and what can be done about excessive, unhealthy
guilt.

Case histories presented for illustrative purposes have, of
course, been disguised to maintain confidentiality; the basic
elements of the experiences of the people involved, however, have
been preserved.

Although all of the opinions in this book are mine, I would
like to express my appreciation to the many authors whose
thoughts have stimulated me. Special thanks are due Dr. Weston
LaBarre and Rabbi Martin Berkowitz. The editing by Jean
Madow was invaluable.

1

Origins of Guilt

In order to understand how to recognize and deal with guilt feelings it is important to be aware of the origins of guilt. An even more basic question is: Do we need a sense of guilt at all? Wouldn't we all be better off if we had no feelings of guilt? As we shall see, healthy guilt serves an extremely important function.

Many factors are involved in the development of a sense of guilt. Basically, guilt arises from four main sources: evolution, religion, law, and the psychological and emotional development of the child. Before considering these, an important distinction should be made between guilty fear and true guilt.

Guilty fear is seen in those individuals who fear they will be caught and punished. They feel little guilt about the act itself. Should they be apprehended and chastised, that is the end of it as far as they are concerned, and they no longer think about it. True guilt, on the other hand, stems from our own internalized standards of behavior. If we believe we have done something wrong, we feel guilty even if we are never caught. If we have been apprehended and punished or have made retribution for the wrongdoing, we often continue to feel guilty. Children develop a sense of guilty fear first, and then later, after acquiring a conscience, they develop true guilt. In tracing the development of a sense of guilt historically, we find that there is a similar developmental pattern, first guilty fear and then, later, a true sense of guilt.

Evolution

When we explore the chronological unfolding of a sense of guilt, we discover that it is basic to the evolution of the human animal.

11

Although one might wonder what possible role guilt could play in the survival of the species, threads of the importance of guilt in the evolutionary process are woven throughout the human fabric.

A number of sciences examine evolution from their various points of view. Paleontologists study fossil remains to establish human ancestry and along with archaeologists, are also interested in the history of human culture. Physical anthropologists focus on the physical structures of humans and their close relatives. When one thinks of Darwin's *Evolution of the Species,* one usually thinks of the physical sciences. However, the social sciences have also made fundamental contributions to the study of evolution.

The anthropologist LaBarre (1959) states succinctly:

> *As they evolved, animals became competitive (for food) and* **had to develop ways and means of getting along with each other, or chaos would result, and the species would not survive** (author's emphasis).

Sociologists and anthropologists have suggested that systems of moral law have evolved culturally as a necessary means of adapting to the vicissitudes of our environment. Along with biological evolution, social thinkers proposed a social evolution known as Social Darwinism. It was used to explain the evolution of marriage and the family as well as other social institutions.

Psychologist Helen Lewis (Tuttman et al. 1981) says

> *Everywhere anthropologists have looked, they have found human beings organized with a society ruled by cultural laws governing the interactions of its members. These cultural laws clearly invade every moment of an individual's experience from birth to burial ceremonies.*

Where cultural laws have evolved for the purpose of survival of the species, there must also develop a sense of right and wrong behavior, which, in turn, would establish a feeling of guilt if we do wrong.

We also developed types of behavior that would allow us to live in peace with our neighbors. We did not steal another's food or mate. If we did, it could lead to mortal combat, and none of us would survive.

We developed a sense of "right" behavior, which would allow for our survival, and "wrong" behavior, which could be fatal and, therefore, was a behavior to be feared. As our sense of right and wrong evolved, we developed a feeling of guilty fear if we did the wrong thing. We learned to cooperate with each other. If we had an excess of food, we not only fed our family but also shared with our neighbors, who in turn, reciprocated when they had additional provisions. We learned to hunt together and protect one another. We invented new tools and weapons to ensure survival.

Unfortunately, we have been so successful in devising new weapons that we are in danger of destroying our own species, a travesty on the purpose of these tools in the first place, which was survival.

Thomas H. Huxley (1898), the renowned English biologist, related the beginnings of conscience to survival. He pointed out that people have an "innate desire to enjoy the pleasures and to escape the pains of life." They desire to do only those things that please them regardless of the effect on society.

"That is their inheritance," says Huxley, "from the long series of ancestors, human and semi-human, and brutal, in whom the strength of this innate tendency to self-assertion was the condition of victory in the struggle for existence."

He made it clear, however, that although the drive for pleasure is one of the essential conditions in our battle with nature, it would lead to the destruction of society if allowed free play. Huxley then pointed out that the need for limiting uncontrolled, totally self-indulged actions is essential for the survival of the family as well, because of the prolonged infancy of the human species. He introduced another term for conscience, calling it "the ethical process."

It is interesting to note that Huxley cautioned against developing too strict a conscience, indicating that self-assertion, within reason, is essential for maintaining a social structure against the demands of nature, but that too much self-restraint can be destructive.

The suggestion, then, is that we all have a conscience that is fundamental and that without it society could not have survived. By Darwin's laws of evolution, this conscience became hereditary. Racial traits are genetically inherited. Cultural traits are socially inherited.

Humans had to develop a sense of right and wrong in their culture to survive. From this beginning, they had to evolve some reaction within themselves if they did something wrong, which could well have been the primordial beginnings of a sense of guilt.

Cultural anthropologists suggest that there are at least three purposes for the development of a sense of guilt for survival. The first is to control the aggressive competitive drives so that a modus vivendi is developed and the human animal does not annihilate itself. The second is to control unbridled sexual behavior so that the family unit is preserved, again permitting survival of the species. The third source for a sense of guilt arises from the prolonged infantilization of the child, who must please his or her parents (that is, be aware of what is "right" behavior and what is "wrong" behavior in their eyes and develop a sense of guilt regarding wrong behavior) in order to survive biologically.

In an evolutionary sense, then, guilt, beginning with guilty fear, was essential at first for the survival of *Homo sapiens* and then for the various societies into which humans organized themselves.

The institution of marriage evolved as a means of insuring survival in our society. Sometimes, however, it boomerangs. Here are two similar stories of people disabled by their unhealthy guilt about marriage.

ARCHIE

Archie, a 35-year-old accountant, was referred because he was unable to concentrate on his work, was losing weight, and felt that life was a "downer." He had a 5-year-old daughter and was struggling with thoughts of divorcing his wife of ten years. His story, briefly, was that when he first met his wife, she was very attractive but firm in her conviction that there was to be no sex before marriage. Archie had had very little experience with sex, but nevertheless succeeded in persuading Anne to go to bed with him. He then felt obligated to marry her and found later that she was not really interested in sex, their home, or developing any kind of a social life. However, Anne did have a good singing voice and was convinced that she would some day sing at the Metropolitan Opera. She spent all her time taking singing lessons and practicing, neglecting the home and Archie. When their little girl was born, Anne couldn't wait to place her in a day-care center. Although Archie was earning a good income, he was unable to save anything because of household expenses. (Anne insisted on frequent cleaning help, the costly singing lessons, and then the day-care center.)

Realizing how unhappy he was in the marriage, he contemplated divorce but found he was unable to initiate it. "She has given me ten years of her life," he said when he discussed it, "and I couldn't leave the child. If I left, how would Anne manage? My father had an unhappy marriage and he put up with it, so I guess I can, too. I would just feel too guilty if I walked out." He felt he had no right to be angry with his wife and when, on occasion, he did explode, he felt ashamed and guilty afterward.

STEPHANIE

Stephanie was a 42-year-old housewife who also was in an unhappy marriage and felt trapped. She had married the most sought-after man in her high school class and felt she was indeed fortunate. Shortly thereafter, he was found to have a testicular tumor and the treatment for it made him sterile. He was still able to have sexual relations but lost interest, preferring to sit up late at night reading and snacking. He gained a great deal of weight, but Stephanie continued to make herself attractive and made all sorts of efforts to entice him early to bed with very little success. Since they were unable to have children of their own, when his sister was killed in an auto accident they adopted her three small children. Stephanie now had the burden of caring for them, and found very little satisfaction in the marriage itself. She began developing stomach pains, became moody, had difficulty getting out of bed in the morning, and had rare, but explosive, temper outbursts.

When I asked her how she felt about her marriage, she said, "Well, my husband can't help himself. It's not his fault that he developed a tumor. If you are wondering why I haven't left him, I would feel too guilty. He means well, and now with the children I couldn't do anything to upset their home. How could I live with myself?"

Although there are many reality factors in these two stories, both Archie and Stephanie were suffering from unhealthy excessive guilt reactions to their anger at being caught in these situations, a guilt they felt was not justified and therefore repressed. Trying to live up to their ideals of the good husband and wife made them feel guilty when they considered doing anything for their own happiness. That would be selfish. The result, of course, was that everyone was unhappy. Archie and Stephanie had first to recognize their guilt feelings and their anger and then deal with both.

As society developed and became more complex, guilt about infanticide, patricide, incest, and adultery had to develop or the family as such would have disappeared.

This first guilt was probably not guilt as we think of it today, related to internalized standards of behavior; it was more comparable to the guilty fear of children who control their behavior because of direct fear of punishment. The higher standards of guilt came later.

Religion

As our awareness of the world around us increased, with its many unknown and threatening aspects, thunder and lightning, floods, destructive fires, and famine, we came to feel that there must be some superior being or beings who were responsible for these various threats of nature and who had to be recognized and dealt with. Religions were born, gods were identified.

At first, these religions dealt chiefly with matters between the people and their gods. If harm befell us, we believed we had offended our gods, and we devised ways for appeasing them. A stronger, more complicated sense of right and wrong with its accompanying guilty fear became a part of our character. If our crops did not grow or our child became ill, we felt we had offended the gods in some way and were being punished for our transgression; but it was not clear what these offenses were, and we felt unable to prevent the recurrence of the catastrophe. More elaborate codes of behavior, which, when violated, were seen as angering the gods, had to be developed so that a clearer cause of right and wrong could be established and be protective, and in a sense allow for survival. If specific ways of worshiping (and thereby appeasing) these gods could be elucidated, a person would know "the right thing to do" and could live a full, peaceful life.

The search for security and protection reached its peak in the exacting rituals of the priests of various religions in preparing and offering their sacrifices to the gods. The priests were considered to be people with extraordinary powers. Some were thought to be descendants of gods and, therefore, to be blindly obeyed. If their commands were violated, guilty fear was generated. Their rules eventually became a part of the Bible, and a more refined sense of right and wrong evolved, now leading to a concept of sin.

In addition to the need to placate the gods in an effort to control natural forces, we found we had to develop ways of living with our neighbors. As societies developed and we began living more and more in groups, it became necessary to establish some rules of behavior, beyond the most primitive, for people to live together in harmony and survive. The codes of behavior of the most primitive tribes that have been studied were transitional to the well-organized religions we know today. These included many rituals and taboos that involved guilt. So powerful were these taboos that if someone transgressed or violated a taboo that was thought to lead to death, the person would actually die out of guilt and fear.

Many examples have been reported. Frazier (1947) tells of a New Zealander who found the unfinished dinner of a high-ranking chief and proceeded to eat it. When this man, who was known for his courage and bravery in the wars of the clan, was told he had eaten the chief's food (a tribal taboo), he developed stomach cramps and convulsed until he died.

As societies evolved, the religious leaders were aware of this need for controls, and they developed codes of ethical and moral behavior. In order for these rules to be accepted and obeyed, however, they had to be seen as originating from an all-powerful Supreme Being. It is not a coincidence that the first three of the Ten Commandments, probably the most basic code of behavior we have, pertain to the establishment of the supremacy of God. Once His power was established as absolute, His decrees became mandatory; and if they were not followed, severe punishment would result.

With the ever-growing categories of rights and wrongs dictated by the gods, there were more and more rules to obey. Violation of the rules became a sin, and we had the beginnings of guilt.

It would take another volume to delineate the development of concepts of sin and guilt in the various religions. Let us examine one example of the differences.

An interesting divergence is seen in the attitude of the Jewish and Christian theologies toward sex. The Old Testament encourages marriage and sexuality in marriage: "It is not good for man to be alone. I shall make him a helpmate" (Genesis 2:18) and "Therefore, a man shall leave his father and mother and cleave only unto his wife, and they shall become as one flesh" (Genesis 2:24).

In the developing Christian tradition, however, celibacy became a goal, and marriage was treated as an unworthy concession to the weakness of the human will. Derrick S. Bailey (1959), an Anglican scholar, writes:

> *The reaction to the Greek and Roman hedonism and sensuality probably led to the later idealization of asceticism which expressed itself primarily in renunciation of sex, wedlock, and the family.*

He points out that stoicism tended to reject marriage, and neopythagoreanism idealized abstinence and regarded sex as a defilement.

> *The virgin state was accorded a supremacy which the Orthodox Jew would have repudiated as an impious frustration of the purposes of God.*

Noonan (1965) felt that the teaching of the value of virginity represented one of the New Testament's major breakaways from the Old Testament.

David M. Feldman (1974) describes Pope Gregory's view of the evils of sexual intercourse.

> *The delectation incidental even to lawful intercourse is always sinful; how much more so when the couple's dominant motive is not procreational.*

Feldman points out that St. Thomas Aquinas located the "seed of coital evil" in what he regarded as the act's inevitable irrationality. Coital pleasure was not sinful as such, but it could not be pursued for its own sake without sin. Within marriage, the sin was always venial; outside marriage it was mortal.

Despite the Protestant Reformation, Martin Luther continued the old concept of the original transgression of Adam and Eve with its resultant punishment. Luther believed that coitus could not be performed without being accompanied by a sense of guilt: "Somehow it is always unclean." Calvin, too, believed that the pleasure of sex was evil.

It comes as no surprise then that despite the increasing liberalization of our attitudes, sex persists today as one of the major sources of guilt.

The basic religious precepts about sex, then, can be understood as a means of protecting the family and prohibiting uninhibited gratification. When they lead to excessive preoccupation with prohibitions against natural feelings, they can cause unhealthy guilt and become harmful.

The puritanical concept that any pleasure was sinful was humorously reported during World War II. The Chief Rabbi for the U.S. Armed Forces was asked, "If a Jewish soldier is caught in the front lines and the only food available is pork chops [forbidden food to Jews], is it a sin if the soldier eats them?" The rabbi's answer was a classic. "The law is clear," he said. "If the food is necessary for survival, of course, he may eat it, but he must not suck on the bones!" The sin is in the enjoyment.

When religion was born, we were just emerging from "barbarian infancy." There were two major areas that required controls. One was the natural elements. The dangers of fire and famine and the need for rain for our crops made us feel that there must be some Supreme Being who had to be placated in order for us to succeed against these forces of nature. The second was the social environment. Guidelines were needed so that we could live in a society in which we could function with our fellow humans effectively. As Joshua Liebman (1946) said:

> The primary needs of religion were the acquisition of the high ideals of monogamy, family fidelity, brotherly compassion, and social righteousness in a world still incapable of distinguishing clearly between right and wrong. The relief one could attain from feeling that there was a higher being to which one could appeal and seek relief from the overwhelming tragedies of nature was tremendous.

Religion has given us important useful codes of behavior aimed at improving our relationships with each other, but at a price. At first, these codes created guilty fear; later through organized early religious training, these rules became an intrinsic part of our character, contributing to the development of a conscience, something from which we could never separate ourselves and which became the generator of true guilt. These religious rules, however, were not sufficiently elaborated to deal with the increasingly complex functioning of our societies, and laws evolved.

Laws

The great religions developed their codes of behavior as set down by a Supreme Being; disobeying these canons led to guilt and fear. Laws developed from a different source, adding to the rules and regulations of expected conduct, violation of which generated guilty fear and, in many, true guilt.

Laws were established so that people would get along with each other, socially and with civility, and in some organized fashion. Some of the religious codes dealt with this need as well, and religion and law became intertwined. Their purpose was to help society function smoothly and effectively.

Edmunds (1959), in his fine distinctive style, tells a story of two desert-island castaways to illustrate the need for law arising out of the need for survival. I recommend Edmunds' *Law and Civilization* both for its lucid style and the clarity with which he derives the origin of laws. In essence, he indicates that if a single castaway is on an island, there is no problem about sharing. But let another castaway land on the same island and concerns for survival arise.

If these castaways were only animals, when cause for provocation arose, they would doubtless fight it out, and the strongest would dominate from then on, if he did not kill the other. In a crude sense, the manifested practice in the animal kingdom that the stronger dominates might be itself thought of as law. In fact, we sometimes hear references as to "The Law of the Jungle."

Edmunds points out that by having rules and working together, we have a better chance of success than if each goes his or her own way. This applies to individuals, families, and the organization of cities, states, and countries. He goes on to describe the need for a conscience and civilization.

Coming back to the castaways, we may reasonably assume that this element (a conscience), innate in our two castaways, would assert itself in the hypothetical situation which we are considering. There would come mutual realization that in the long run each would be better off to have a companion to make common cause against the difficulties and dangers of the environment.

Edmunds indicates that with the development of a mutual understanding, each castaway would respect the life and property of the other. He defines law as the "rule of ordered conduct" and points out that law was established to preserve society's interest in general security.

Edmunds speaks of conscience as that part of us that allows us to separate out what is just and right. He does not speak of the concern people develop if their conscience tells them they have done something wrong. A sense of guilt contributes to the ability of the conscience to distinguish right from wrong. This is healthy guilt.

As long as muggers on the street are not afraid of being caught, they will attack their victims with no remorse and feel no guilt about it. Laws in themselves will not stop this type of behavior. Healthy guilt (or remorse) is essential in those who violate society's laws. The survival of our society depends on it.

How to deter people from misbehaving and how to make them obey the laws has been a problem since ancient times. Kings must have understood this long ago when they ruled both as the supreme commanders of the state and either as descendants of the gods or by "divine right" given them by the gods. The deified leader reinforced the guilty fear as he threatened punishment both by the state in this life and by the gods in the hereafter.

The whole issue of what constitutes effective punishment is far from settled. The most successful punishment prescribed for the violation of law is the one that stirs up the greatest amount of guilty fear or, even more, stimulates the conscience and generates true guilt. In most cases, when people break a law and are not apprehended, such as by speeding or by using marijuana or drinking, they do not dwell on it and are not troubled by it. Their consciences do not become involved. However, where such offenses have clearly led to harming other persons, their consciences may then begin to torment them depending on the strength of the standards built into the consciences.

There are studies that indicate that laws prescribing severe punishment do not usually deter hardened criminals. Laws usually influence the law-abiding citizen. This is probably related to the fact that the criminal has a different set of standards, or a paucity of them, in his or her conscience compared with the law-abiding citizen.

People react to law in several ways. Ideally, they should understand that the purpose of the law is to make society function efficiently. It should make sense and they should want to obey it. If they obey it because they are afraid they will be caught and punished—this is guilty fear. If they conform to the law because they know it is wrong to break the law, regardless of the possibility of being apprehended—this is true guilt. The stronger one's conscience, the more one may feel compelled to conform rigorously to the letter of the law. Laws contribute to guilt by establishing standards accepted by individuals as part of their consciences.

How does the conscience develop?

2

Origins of Conscience

Evolution, religion, and law are the three major sources of codes of behavior. These give us established standards by which all of us are expected to live in order to function successfully in our society.

How do these principles become a part of our character? How and by whom are they inculcated as an integral portion of our psychic structure so that we take them with us wherever we go and we are aware of them even if no one else is? We develop a conscience. It arises chiefly from the interaction with one's parents and other figures of authority in one's life.

A 32-year-old stockbroker reported that whenever he has to say "No" he feels guilty. Recalling his childhood, he said that he still remembers the fire in his mother's eyes as she said, "Don't you dare say 'no' to me!"

"It scared the hell out of me," he declared. "I wonder if that has anything to do with the guilt I feel now?"

Most psychological theories also indicate that the ultimate source of the conscience is biological. The conscience serves an important function in the lengthy duration of a person's childhood. Psychologists also suggest that the development of conscience has something to do with survival and is thus related to the other theories of evolution, religion, and law. The survival in the case of the helpless child, however, is related to the relationship with the parents and the need to retain their love and not be punished.

The conscience contains not only the external standards set by our parents and society but also the prohibitions against desires and wishes that we all have and that, unless restrained, would make it impossible to survive in a civilized society. The latter concept is by no means a recent discovery. Socrates commented on this situation over 2,000 years ago. In describing the Tyrannic Man, he indicated that some of our desires and pleasures are lawless but that we all have them. With laws and reason we can usually control them, but they continue to exist and come out in sleep.

> *Whenever the rest of the soul, all the reasonable, gentle, and ruling part is asleep, the bestial and savage part tries to go and fulfill its own instincts.*
>
> *There is nothing it will not dare to do, thus freed and rid of all shame and reason, it shrinks not from attempting in fancy to lie with a mother, or with any other man or god or beast, shrinks from no bloodshed, refrains from no food—in a word, leaves no folly or shamelessness untried.*

This was written 2,000 years before Sigmund Freud's *Interpretation of Dreams* (1910).

Authorities differ regarding the timing of the emergence of conscience. Some, like Melanie Klein, a British psychoanalyst, feel that it begins very early in life. Klein suggests that even 6-month-old infants have ideas of a "good me" and a "bad me" as well as a "good world" and a "bad world."

Most theories are variations of Freud's ideas about the development of the superego, a concept usually used synonymously with conscience. Freud began by differentiating between an ego ideal and a superego. In his later writings, he tended to use the two interchangeably. His concept of the ego ideal was that it came from an idealization and a sense of the omnipotence of the parents; that is, the ego ideal is the kind of behavior for which we all strive. We consider it the perfect type of behavior. In a discussion of morals and emotional illness (1908), Freud said,

> *All who wish to reach a higher standard than their constitution will allow will fall victim to neurosis. It would have been better for them if they had remained "less perfect."*

The idea of the formation of the ego ideal rests upon another mechanism: identification. The little boy wishes to grow up to be like his father, the little girl like her mother.

Shame and guilt have been distinguished by whether we are responding to our ego ideal or to our superego. As Piers and Singer (1953) point out, when we do something that is against our ego ideal, we feel shame. If it is against our superego, we feel guilt. Shame leads to a fear of abandonment by our parents, guilt to a fear of punishment and injury.

Helen Lewis (1971) describes the distinction in parental terms:

> *Identification with the beloved or admired ego-ideal (parents) stirs pride and triumphant feelings; failure to live up to this internalized admired image stirs an "internalized threat" which is experienced as guilt.*

Lewis indicates that shame focuses on the evolution of one's self. A defeat in competition or a sexual rebuff leads to shame. In guilt, the person is not the central focus but rather the thing that was done or undone. Words such as "embarrassment," "humiliation," "mortification," and "chagrin" are frequently used in association with shame. Guilt is more involved with feelings of having done something wrong.

Erik Erickson (1968) describes shame as:

> *an infantile emotion insufficiently studied because in our civilization it is so early and easily absorbed by guilt.*

He equates shame with being looked at and indicates that being self-conscious is related to the feeling of shame. Often in dreams portraying shame we are only partially clothed, exposed "with one's pants down."

Erickson relates the sense of shame to the period of learning to control one's bodily functions and cautions that too much shaming can be harmful and lead to rebellious behavior that is deliberately shameless. Guilt, says Erickson, develops around the oedipal period, similar to Freud's concept. It is related to the development of masculine and feminine traits in the child and especially sexual interests. These, in turn, lead to exciting but frightening fantasies. "A deep sense of guilt is awakened, a strange sense; for it seems forever to imply that the individual actually has committed crimes and deeds that were, after all, not only not committed but would have been biologically quite impossible."

Erickson goes on to describe the rivalry that develops between the child and the parent of the opposite sex and observes that the harsh, unyielding conscience can restrict initiative. But he adds an optimistic note:

> *There is little in these inner developments which cannot be harnessed to constructive and peaceful initiative if we learn to understand the conflicts and anxieties of childhood and the importance of childhood for mankind.*

This is one of the most important observations to be made in this book. Our guilt feelings are not necessarily written in stone. Once we have a better understanding of where these feelings come from and how they are formed, *they can be modified.*

As we grow older, particularly when we enter adolescence, we tend to devalue the ego ideal concepts set up by our parents, just as we tend to devalue our parents themselves. This is probably why the adolescent goes through such a rebellious period in which it seems that nothing the parent does is right; peer pressure moves in, and now the adolescent has a new set of values.

Perhaps the biggest factor in the development of the superego and conscience, however, is the struggle that we go through around the age of 3 or 4, trying to resolve our feelings toward our father and mother.

Although many analysts still feel that the beginning of the development of conscience really gets underway at age 3 or 4, there is evidence now that roots for the conscience are established much earlier. H. Blum describes this process in "Superego Formation, Adolescent Transformation and the Adult Neurosis" (1983). He points out that the precursors for conscience are laid down within the first year of life as the child begins to separate from his or her mother and sees her as a separate person. The child becomes aware of the need to please this important separate individual and begins to learn those things of which she approves and those she does not.

The conscience, then, has its beginnings in our earliest years, as we attempt to meet the standards and the prohibitions of our parents and care-taking authorities.

Child psychoanalysts speak of oral guilt and anal guilt developing in these early years. Oral guilt refers to the child's wish to bite and devour everything and Mother says, "No, No!" Children soon learn that biting is a no-no and withhold their desire to bite, feeling guilty if they do bite. Similarly, anal guilt develops as a result of the child's wish to play with his or her feces and smear it around. It's such fun! Again, Mother says, "No, No!" but the desire persists. Knowing it is now a no-no when the wish is indulged, the child develops anal guilt. One of the early analysts, Sandor Ferenzi, referred to the effects of this anal stage of development of our conscience as "anal morality."

During these formative years, however, the factors contributing to the child's sense of conscience are chiefly related to people in the environment. When these people are not around, the child does not as yet have a strong internalized conscience; that is, we have not developed within ourselves the full conscience that comes later in life and becomes a part of our personality. We therefore tend to behave much more freely when our parents are not around. Our only concern is not to do something our parents might find out about and of which they may disapprove. This has been called "social anxiety" or "guilty fear" and is still not a fully developed conscience but rather a fear of punishment. There are in it, however, the beginnings of a conscience.

Another means of dealing with these forbidden wishes is to find substitutions. Children love to mess up and play with food, such as mushy cereals. Later they make mud pies and smear paints with their fingers.

Around age 3 or 4, we begin to develop the true internalized standards of conscience that become a part of us for the rest of our lives, with additions and modifications particularly through adolescence and extending into adult life. It is during this time that we develop strong sexual feelings toward the parent of the opposite sex and powerful negative feelings toward the parent of the same sex. But there is a sense also that these are very dangerous wishes and that these big people would not approve of them. We protect ourselves by identifying with the parents, saying in essence, "I don't approve of these wishes either," and we then become like our parents in declaring that these wishes are *bad*.

We try to control our sexual and murderous impulses toward our parents by developing a conscience, which says that these things are wrong, harmful, and forbidden, because we feel they are dangerous and must be denied. The conscience has a large component directed toward our own inner desires. Curiously enough, the stronger the murderous and sexual feelings are, the stronger the conscience has to be to fight them, so that the person who has the strictest superego or conscience may very well be the person who has the strongest sexual and aggressive impulses. The aggressive drive may then be turned against one's self so that now the superego contains an instinctual drive, a destructive one, which strengthens the need for punishment demanded by the superego.

In his short story "Rain," Somerset Maugham describes a missionary, the Reverend Davidson, who is driven to try to save the soul of a prostitute. He is making progress, and she is beginning to change her behavior, when one morning he is found dead, having committed suicide after he succumbs to his own sexual desires, against which he has been fighting so fiercely in his missionary work with others. His strict conscience forbade his indulging his strong natural sexual drive; he, therefore, became a missionary who spent his life trying to make others repress it too. When he was overwhelmed with temptation by the prostitute and gave in to his wish, his guilt was so strong that he killed himself. The prostitute summarizes all of this in her statement at the end of the story: "You men are all alike!"

In general, we react most severely to those "forbidden" situations that are most tempting to us. In the days of Prohibition, the teetotalers who went around the saloons striking drinkers with their umbrellas turned out to have very strong desires for alcohol themselves. They were fighting against it by proclaiming loudly their total opposition to alcohol.

The latent homosexual who is accosted by a homosexual becomes overly upset, concerned, and sometimes violent because the invitation is too close to his or her own wish. He or she disapproves of and has repressed those feelings and must, therefore, overreact in an effort to deny them.

A young psychiatric resident told this story: He had been treating a young man who indicated an attraction for him. One day the patient declared that he would like to have a sexual affair with him. The doctor said he became lightheaded and felt as if he were going to faint. He had to excuse himself and leave the room until he could pull himself together. The doctor said to me, "I can't understand what happened. I had been fighting off a cold. Could it have been the virus?" After discussion, he was encouraged to consider other possibilities.

The superego or conscience, then, arises from our images of our parents and their standards, which we take into and make a part of ourselves; this becomes a part of our own personalities so that later, whether the parents are present or not, it is constantly with us. This is the essence of conscience. The process has been described not only as an issue of individual survival but also as an important part of the survival of the civilization as well, thus tying it in with social and anthropological concepts.

In *Civilization and Its Discontents,* Freud (1920) describes the struggle between the strict superego and the ego which results in a sense of guilt. He points out that the reason for developing this sense of good or bad arises from our helpless feelings as a child and our awareness of our need to rely on the important adults in our life, with a fear of antagonizing them and losing their love. One of the child's chief concerns is the danger that this stronger person will show his or her superiority by punishing the child.

Unfortunately, the large number of cases of child abuse now being reported make this more than a theoretical concept. The strange thing is that the child abuser frequently has a history of having been abused himself. One would think that these mistreated children would be especially kind to their offspring, but unfortunately their anger and resentment is released when they are adults and model themselves on their parents, identifying with the aggressor.

The timing of the origin of conscience has been confirmed by other studies. Inspired by the pioneering Swiss psychologist Jean Piaget, cognitive psychologists have been observing the development of feelings chronologically and report that children at birth may show pleasure, disgust, and distress. Within weeks one can see joy in their reactions. Anger develops in the next three to four months, sadness and fear four or five months later, and shame by one-and-a-half years of age. It is not until the child is 3 or 4 years old that one observes manifestations of true guilt.

A more sophisticated sense of guilt develops a few years later. An article on excuses in the *New York Times* (1984) quotes developmental psychologists who have identified stages in children's use of excuses.

The excuses pre-school children make are usually flimsy. They need to protect their self-image (shame), and the ability to make sophisticated excuses does not ordinarily emerge until six to nine years.

The child does not fully develop a sophisticated sense of guilt until after age 6. The theory connects the development of image-protecting excuses to the evolvement of self-criticism during those years of life.

The author distinguishes between the 6-year-old who is

critical of a friend's behavior but not his own and a 7-year-old who begins to worry about what other people might think. By the time he becomes 8 years of age, the child is struggling with trying to meet his or her own standards. Excuses then develop in an effort to relieve the guilt arising in the child from not having met those standards.

In the beginning, what is bad is whatever we think or do that might cause us to lose our parents' love or to be punished. The danger sets in only if and when the authority discovers the bad act or thought. There are some people who continue to function this way all their lives. They will allow themselves to do anything "bad" that promises them enjoyment so long as they believe the authorities will not find out about it or blame them for it. They function only through the fear of being discovered and punished.

When Bobby was 7 years old, his father, knowing nothing of what had really happened that day, teased him by saying, "I heard what you did today!" Bobby immediately launched into a long story about being accused of punching Johnny, and that he really had only tapped him, and only because Johnny hit him first. When his father told him that he really hadn't known about it, Bobby was humiliated, felt guilty—and was furious.

During that crucial state when, as children, we develop strong sexual and aggressive feelings toward our parents, we must deal more specifically, not only with the outside authority whose love we want and whom we fear, but also with our own internal wishes, which are very exciting and very frightening because these authority figures would not approve and would punish us severely if they knew. In order to deal with these problems, we assume their standards and make them a part of ourselves. Anna Freud refers to this development as "identification with the aggressor." Many of us do deal with our fears by identifying with the aggressor. A number of Germans became Nazis out of fear of Hitler and his band of hoodlums and felt they were safer by identifying with the Nazis and acting as one of them.

A pivotal change takes place when the authority of our

parents is internalized through the establishment of the conscience or superego, which then becomes a part of our own personality. At this point, the distinction between doing something bad and wishing to do it disappears, since nothing can now be hidden from the superego, not even our own thoughts. From here on, anything of which our conscience disapproves can make us feel guilty, and we take our conscience with us wherever we go. True guilt feelings come from the internal disapproval of a wish or act measured against our own conscience.

Some men patients have said that they feel they are just like their fathers, and they hate it because they say they do not really like their fathers. They are completely unaware of the fact that they have been identifying with their fathers out of fear and because they want their father's love. Similarly, women have spoken of being just like their mothers and resenting it in themselves, confirming that it is an unconscious influence over which they have no conscious control. Often during adolescence, there is a strong rebellion against this built-in parent. In most of us this rebellion does not last.

It is not uncommon to hear people say as they are getting older, "I seem to be getting more and more like my father [or my mother] all the time." One man said, "I hate my father for what he did to me. I find myself acting more and more like him every day, and I feel he did that to me. I resent it because he set the example, and I behave just like him. I hate the person, yet I can't seem to help myself."

These feelings can be relieved if one recognizes and accepts that it is no longer necessary to be like one's parent either out of fear or to gain approval.

An interesting variation that occurs in some of us is a sense of guilt if we are more successful than our parents. It has been called "the Vice-President Syndrome." A man who is very comfortable in a low management position does so well that he is promoted to be vice president. He then becomes depressed. One reason is that he is not comfortable with being more successful than his father. Comedian Sid Caesar in his biography points out that one of the chief reasons for his drinking was his great guilt feeling about having surpassed his father.

There is a marked difference between the fear of punishment and true guilt, and each must be dealt with differently. We all have a fear of punishment, and we all do things that might even be illegal but have no concern about it as long as we believe we will not be caught. Very few people, for example, would be upset if they received all of their money back in a phone booth after making a call. They would have very little, if any, guilt about it and, in fact, might actually enjoy it because they would feel they were "getting away with something." We rationalize that since the phone company is a big impersonal corporation that makes lots of money, the loss of a few coins would not be significant. How often do we exceed the speed limit, thus breaking the law, and feel no guilt about it? We forget that the law is for our own as well as others' safety, and when a policeman pulls us over to give us a ticket, we get furious with him because we know we are guilty. Often we try to rationalize by wondering (necessarily to ourselves) why he is not spending his time more usefully catching all the murderers and thieves who are getting away with their crimes. Rarely do most of us feel guilty about speeding as long as we get away with it.

Guilt pertains to feeling that we have done something wrong according to our own conscience, even though it ultimately is a fear of punishment or was originally derived from that fear. The punishment is built into our character so that if we feel we have violated our own standards, we tend to punish ourselves with feelings of anxiety and rage against ourselves, upbraiding ourselves, sometimes literally inflicting physical pain in an effort to punish ourselves and thus relieve the guilt feelings.

A recent newspaper headline in the *Philadelphia Inquirer* (February 24, 1985) states: "Guilt Led a Troubled Woman to Confess." The article goes on to say that Audrey Burford could have gotten away with murder. She had, indeed, killed her boyfriend, but no one had any reason to suspect her. Five years later she confessed. The authorities apparently were not even aware that a murder had taken place.

She said, "I knew in my heart and mind that I was guilty."

In prison the other women said to her, "You're an ass! You turned yourself in."

"But," she protested, "if you never killed anyone, you don't know what it is to feel guilt in your heart.

"From the night of the murder until I turned myself in," she explained, "I fought to keep it out of my mind with drinking and with drugs. I drank so much that I would have blackouts, but they hadn't made enough of either (drugs or alcohol) to make me forget. I didn't think I was worthy of my children. That was part of the punishment. I tried to escape and forget it," she said, "but there's a time in life when you've got to face the things you've done."

This is true conscience.

Does everyone feel guilty? Yes, with some exceptions, but to different degrees and about different things, depending on what we were taught to believe is right or wrong. A youngster in the ghetto may have no guilt about looting a store damaged in a storm but may feel extreme guilt about not supporting his friend in a fight.

The guilty person suffers from feelings of remorse, feeling sorry that he or she did the act. Sorrow is another factor in a response to feelings of guilt. Humiliation may also be a common reaction or a part of the guilt in the sense that the guilty person feels he or she has done something terrible that reflects on him or her and that therefore acceptance will be withheld. (See Chapter 5, "Narcissistic Guilt.")

R. L. Jenkins (1950) makes an interesting distinction between conscience and superego. "Conscience," he says, "stresses the religious, ethical, and rational elements, whereas superego emphasizes the primitive, infantile, and irrational elements." Most people use the two terms interchangeably. The part of our personality that makes us feel guilty is made up of both our internal unacceptable drives and the standards imposed from the outside by parents, religious teachings, and other authorities.

What do we know about these feelings inside ourselves that can lead to such misery and pain, which we describe as guilt?

3

Guilt and Sex

Once the conscience is developed, it becomes an integral part of our personality that is constantly, critically, judging our thoughts, wishes, and actions. It surveys not only those things of which we are aware but also passes judgment on the contents of our unconscious mind. One of its major functions is to restrain and control our otherwise uninhibited impulses.

What are the desires in our unconscious that are most troublesome? The sexual drive is probably the single most powerful instinctual force in our lives. Despite the changing mores in our society and the so-called sexual revolution which has liberalized our attitudes toward sex, many continue to feel guilty about sexual desires.

There are still taboos associated with sex, derived from religious teachings, from parents, various laws, and other social influences. Some religions have retained a very rigid attitude toward sex and generate excessive guilt in their followers. In a number of orthodox religions, it is still a sin to masturbate, to have sex outside marriage, or to indulge in any variation of sexual activity between consenting partners other than conventional sexual intercourse.

We should all explore our attitudes about sex because they may produce guilt in our children over their sexual desires. If we dress behind closed doors, never allow the children to see us naked, and keep the bedroom door locked at night, the child receives the impression that there is something bad or wrong about sex. If we avoid answering questions about sex, use "cute" substitute names for anatomical parts, and become upset if the child touches his or her genitalia, these attitudes and behaviors can plant seeds of guilt about sex. Children are much more attuned to parental views and responses than is generally realized. Attitudes of peers and other adults may also contribute to feelings about sex. Puritanical standards toward sex still persist in some families.

The association of shame and guilt with sex is found as early as the first writings in the Bible. Adam and Eve, who were naked before they ate the apple from the tree of knowledge, were described as "not ashamed." After they ate of the fruit that gave them knowledge of good and evil, the Bible declares:

The eyes of both of them were opened, and they discovered that they were naked, so they sewed fig leaves together and made themselves loin cloths.

It is told that when God called for Adam, Adam said, "I heard Thy voice in the garden, and I was afraid because I was naked, and I hid myself."

These clear references to the sexual organs as a source of guilt and shame are also heard in the not uncommon expression "They covered their shame," meaning they covered the genitalia.

Being born in sin carries the connotation of the sinfulness of sex, even when it leads to pregnancy. God's curse on woman for having eaten the forbidden fruit also refers to the end result of sex; namely, that she would suffer pain and sorrow at childbirth.

One cannot help notice that one of the basic differences between good and evil pertains to sexual matters and that even thoughts about sex are evil.

Masturbation

As mentioned, although there are more liberal attitudes toward sex today, there continues to be guilt about masturbation for many people who consider it harmful physically as well as mentally. If you masturbate, you have guilt feelings. There are people who feel so guilty about masturbation that each time they do it, they swear they will never do it again, only to find that the drive is so strong they continue. A 40-year-old law partner in a prestigious law firm reported that he is convinced that his feelings of insecurity and need to have everyone like him stem from his guilt over masturbation.

Some years ago I treated a man I will call Steve who was suffering from a severe obsessive–compulsive neurosis and was almost unable to function because of it. He had a hand-washing compulsion; every time he touched something that he thought was contaminated, he was driven to wash his hands immediately. This drive was so intense that some days he washed his hands over 100 times. The skin became raw and although at times he bled because of his constant scrubbing and the exposure to soap, the compulsion persisted. Sometimes it would take him an hour to get dressed in the morning because he had to check each piece of clothing to make sure that there were no spots of dirt on it. He was living a life in which he was almost paralyzed by his obsessions and compulsions.

During the course of his treatment Steve revealed that his obsessional thinking began when he was 12 years old and first masturbated. He had been reared as a strict Catholic and was a well-behaved youngster and a good student, but he was introverted and extremely shy when around girls. He became concerned about masturbation and frequently went to confession for absolution.

He recalled one such episode vividly. The priest had absolved him, but as he was walking out of the church, the sexual thoughts about masturbation returned. He went back to the confessional, feeling guilty because he was having these sexual desires, and the priest absolved him a second time. Again, as he was walking out of the church, the sexual ideas came into his mind. He returned to the confessional a third time. The priest became angry, took him by the collar, and threw him out of the church, saying "Get out, and don't come back here again with those thoughts!" He felt he was condemned forever. Steve had many other problems, but his guilt over masturbation contributed greatly to his neurosis.

There are times when patients will say they never masturbated and be defensive about it. A careful history reveals that they may never have masturbated directly or manually, although often they will tell of the times when they derived pleasure by rubbing up against something. This denial seems to be more common in girls than boys. They may describe great pleasure in sitting on daddy's knee and rubbing up against him, sliding down banisters, or riding horses. This need for denial of masturbation usually stems from the guilt feelings about it.

The "wet dreams" or noctural emissions of boys may also contribute to the guilt and concern about being found out. Some will attempt to hide the evidence by stripping the sheets from the bed and washing them in secret.

There is nothing inherently abnormal or harmful about masturbation. In fact, if someone denies ever having masturbated, it can be considered an emotional problem. Masturbation done to excess or as a 24-hour preoccupation is a problem, not because of physical injury, but because it indicates the person has problems he or she is trying to solve by a means that will not solve them. Lonely people, those who feel unloved, or the young man who is obsessed with his virility may be trying to resolve their emotional problems by consoling themselves through the reassurance of masturbation. The reality is that it not only does not solve the issue but the obsession interferes with healthy living. That is the only harm.

Incest

Some of the most powerful guilt producers about sex in our society pertain to taboos about incest. The Bible discusses incest in great detail, emphasizing its sinfulness.

Dr. D. Renshaw in her book on incest (1982) makes a number of important observations. Incest has been considered by some writers to be the most extreme form of deviant behavior, or the universal crime. Legally it is a felony and morally it is a major sin. Yet there were cultures such as ancient Egypt or the royal families of Hawaii in which marriage within the family was mandated. In some primitive tribes, the practice of incest is carefully regulated by rituals in which specific acts of incest, including marriage between close family members such as brother and sister, cousins, and other relatives, are the norm.

All states of the United State make incestuous fornication or incestuous intermarriage a crime, yet some surveys suggest that as many as 10 percent of individuals may be involved in some form of incest. The numbers are believed to be increasing. Renshaw says:

> *Incestuous desires (attractions) are natural sexual feelings. A variety of unconscious or deliberate mechanisms must be developed to avoid, deny, control, attack, and repress these natural sexual feelings which are real.*

She points out that great emphasis has been placed by old and new religions on controlling the undesirable drives of sex and aggression. These religions insist that sex be used only for procreation.

The child has an interest in an incestuous relationship that is both forbidden and dangerous and must be denied. A revealing example of both the guilt and the pleasure of sex with a parent was told to me by Margaret.

MARGARET

Margaret was a 35-year-old, thrice-married woman, who although not particularly attractive, was animated and sparkling, giving her a great deal of charm. She came to see me because she was having trouble in her third marriage and was afraid that it might also end in divorce. She was clearly anxious and concerned, and wanted to do everything she could to save the marriage. She was a nurse and particularly enjoyed her men patients, especially the older ones. She had no trouble with men in general but was constantly fighting with her husband, saying that he picked an argument at the least provocation. "He is just like my father," she declared.

When I asked her about her family, she freely told the following story: "My father was a tyrant at home, easily moved to temper outbursts. He was very possessive of me, would not let me go out of the house or visit friends. When I was 12, he began molesting me, seeking to fondle me, and attempting other sexual acts but not intercourse."

She said she tried to fight him off but finally decided that the safest thing, since she was afraid of him, was to let him do what he wanted and "get it over with." His particular interest was in having her perform oral sex. She revealed that this had gone on for at least five years when she finally ran away from home to get married.

I asked her how she felt about her father.

She declared with feeling, "I hated him! Yet recently I have been feeling sorry for him, and I even told him I forgive him." She said that she had told no one about this sexual molestation because she felt so guilty and ashamed.

Despite the feelings of guilt that she had about the sexual acts with her father, Margaret admitted that she always like men better than women and did enjoy sex, particularly the kind her father had forced on her. In her first marriage she chose a man just like her father but found him boring and not ambitious. Moreover, like her father, he had a violent temper and was cruel to her. Her second marriage was to a man who was also domineering like her father. They, too, had so many arguments and their relationship was so intolerable, she finally left him. She was now married to a man twenty years her senior, and was becoming bored with him, too. She felt he was a stick-in-the-mud who was only interested in sitting at home, watching television, and drinking beer while she wanted to go out dancing and socializing. When he was intoxicated, he became abusive and demanded that she perform oral sex on him.

Was it coincidence that she married three men who were like

her father and she found that she enjoyed the same type of sex she had when a young girl with her father?

Incestuous wishes can produce enormous amounts of guilt in the participants. Part of this is due to our instinctual wish for incest. Our conscience then attempts to control this desire by strongly condemning it as wrong, and guilt results. Renshaw points out that incestuous desires are natural physiological sexual feelings and one should not feel guilty for having those feelings. Acting them out is another matter. It is similar to the situation with anger. Everyone gets angry with his or her parents at times. Expressing the anger, however, is not usually the best way to deal with the problem. Healthy guilt feelings about expressing the anger will usually help the person use the energy in a more constructive way. So it is with incest. Finding "a girl just like the girl who married dear old Dad" is one healthy outlet for those feelings.

Adolescence

The adolescent struggles with feelings of guilt about sex, and these feelings differ for the boy and the girl. Both may feel guilty about having sexual feelings, but, in addition, the boy is focusing on his need to prove his manliness, whereas the girl is more concerned about whether or not she is attractive and found desirable by the boy.

One rarely hears of a boy asking a girl, "Will you respect me in the morning?" This is of more concern to the girl, who really wants to know, "Will you still love me in the morning?"

On the other hand, there are the recently changing attitudes about sex, particularly the growing feeling among women that women too have the right to enjoy sex — a very desirable change; however, if the woman insists that the man satisfy her and if the man is struggling with his concern about his manliness, such a demand puts him on trial. We now see men, particularly adolescents, who are struggling with their need to prove their manliness to themselves, who are avoiding sexual intercourse or have become impotent as a result of the stress of this situation.

Adult Sex

Many men confuse sex with manliness and may or may not be concerned with whether or not their partners love them. Love usually has a greater significance as part of the sex act to the woman; and despite the pressures for equality, very few women have the attitude about sex that they can take it or leave it. One young woman declared, "My goal is to use men for my purposes, rather than letting them use me!" She is very active sexually with many different partners, and most of the men are delighted to be used. She is not a happy woman, however, and the statement bristles with her hostility toward men.

A young man tells his friend, "There certainly is a lot of sex available in Florida."

"Oh, really?" says his friend. "Did you get much?"

"No," he replied, "but my sister sure did!"

Why is this so funny?

If the man has not resolved his basic psychological need, he will continue to try to prove his manliness, often through a succession of sexual conquests that can create problems if continued into his marriage. He may feel guilty about having sexual desires and not be aware that the problem is basically not a sexual one but a need to prove himself. A number of patients have described their interests in women other than their wives as a challenge; not infrequently, once they have made the conquest, they will say that they quickly lose interest in the sexual act itself.

A number of women are struggling with the confusion they feel since the liberation brought by the sexual revolution. One of the basic problems is the lack of distinction between love and sex (see Madow 1982, Chapter 9).

Women will often quite accurately accuse men of being interested only in sex, whereas they themselves are not primarily focused on that part of the relationship. The woman's interest is more in feeling that the man cares for her and finds her desirable (see Madow 1982, Chapter 2).

Recently, the syndicated columnist Ann Landers conducted a poll in which she asked women readers "Would you be content to be held close and treated tenderly, and forget about 'the act'?" More than 90,000 women responded. One can undoubtedly raise many questions about her research design, but 72 percent of the women who replied said *yes* they would be content to be held close and treated tenderly and forget about the act. This certainly supports the idea that women want to feel lovable and loved. Sex alone does not answer the need.

Despite the changing, more accepting attitude toward sexual freedom, it is my impression that there is still a major difference between the viewpoints of many families toward open sex for the young man and the young woman. It is much more frequent for the family to say to the young man, "If you like her, live with her. Why do you have to marry her?"

One mother of a young man told me, "I can't understand these mothers of the young women who sleep so freely with my son. How can they allow their daughters to do it?" She is totally unaware that she is saying, "It's OK for my son, but the girls should be restricted!"

The posture that sex for young females should be related only to marriage and family still generates guilt about sex in a number of unmarried women. Many parents feel that it should.

Adults may have guilt feelings over sexual interests in younger partners. Although this appears to be more accepted today, many people still consider it shameful for an older man to be interested sexually in a young woman. There are even stronger feelings against an older woman being attracted to a young man. Teachers who become sexually involved with their students are highly disapproved of, and should be, if the teacher is taking advantage of his or her position. The disapproval, however, may also have in it the overtones of the condemnation of an older person's being sexually attracted to a much younger one.

A college professor who has a special interest in dreams and their meanings reported the following dream: "A female student I had taught some years ago was walking toward me. We were on a street, and it was foggy. She was dressed in a nightgown with a coat thrown over her shoulders. She appeared lovely but pale and seemed to be lost.

"I said to her, 'You should not be out on this cold, damp night. Let me take you home.'

"I walked her back to her apartment although she seemed somewhat reluctant. I went into her bedroom and began to undress. When I had only my shorts on, a man came in and announced that he was her father. He was dressed in a tee shirt and shorts. I chatted with him calmly attempting to make conversation. Inwardly, however, I felt guilty, humiliated, embarrassed, and angry at the poor timing. I continued to prattle and casually began to get dressed. As the dream ended, I was fully clothed and ready to leave the apartment."

What does the dream mean? My friend proffered his own interpretation. "Manifestly I was interested in going to bed with this student, but since it is my dream, I arranged to have her father walk in and stop it. I punished myself for having such an idea by feeling embarrassed and mortified, and, of course, seeing to it that nothing happened."

Even in a dream, guilt can stop you from fulfilling your fantasy. After all, a teacher should not have a sexual interest in a student. The professor said that the pupil had developed a schoolgirl crush on him, and he had found her attractive, but the idea that teachers do not take advantage of students had been thoroughly instilled in him. He had been caught literally with his pants down, thus belittling and humiliating himself for having such forbidden desires.

Sexual wishes need not create pathological guilt feelings. We all have such desires. The important questions are why we have them for a particular partner and what we do about them. The woman who is attracted to older men as sexual partners may feel that they are more mature and considerate or she may be confusing adult sexuality with a little girl's love for her father. The Don Juan who must have sex with every woman he meets may be trying to prove something to himself through these conquests. Fenichel (1974) believed that an excessive preoccupation with sex is an indication of a problem that needs to be resolved and should not lead to guilt feelings.

If one can understand the emotional issues behind the fixation, one is in a better position to deal with the problem.

ROSE

Rose came to see me because she felt she was so obsessed with sex that it was, as she said, "driving me crazy." Rose was a 32-year-old married woman who worked as a secretary in a law office, and her best friend was Anne, a receptionist in the same office. Anne was attracted to Rose's boss and began having an affair with him. She confided this to Rose, and Rose said she had been unable to think about anything else since.

When Anne first told Rose about it, Rose tried to talk her out of it, telling her that after all she was a married woman, and besides office affairs interfere with the efficient functioning of the business. Anne said she couldn't help it, she found him exciting and proceeded with the affair. Rose was distraught. She felt agitated, anxious, and developed palpitations.

"I must be some kind of a sex fiend. All I can think about is the two of them together in bed having a great time!" It did not take very much probing to find out that Rose was also attracted to her boss. Since she was married, she could not allow herself to consider that she might have sexual feelings about him. She resented Anne because she appeared to have no guilt about it and felt free to act on her feelings.

Rose was married to an engineer who was a troubleshooter for his company and traveled a great deal. She was certain he was having sex with other women, and although he denied it when confronted, he did say it was lonely away from home. She had had fleeting thoughts of having an affair of her own to get back at him but dismissed them. Her boss was kind, sensitive, and affectionate. Rose idolized him. At first she denied any sexual interest in him but admitted she wished her husband were more like him.

Rose thought her problem was her preoccupation with sex; but in reality it was much more related to her unhappy marriage, her wish for love and affection from her boss, and her feelings of resentment toward her friend Anne. Rose admitted that having a sexual affair with her boss would not solve her problems. She would have felt too guilty about it. She needed to work on her unhappy marriage and her feelings of betrayal by her friend.

Homosexuality

An interest in homosexuality may generate excessive guilt feelings. The person who is actively homosexual, who has accepted it as his or her sexual orientation, and who is comfortable with that lifestyle does not need to feel guilty about it. Most people, however, are very uncomfortable with homosexual feelings and suffer tremendous guilt over such interests. The guilt may be so powerful and frightening that it is repressed, and the person is not aware either of the homosexual feelings or the guilt. If a situation arises that threatens to expose the homosexual wishes, as for instance, in being approached sexually by a homosexual, the person becomes so frightened that he or she might reveal his or her own unacceptable repressed homosexual feelings, the person overreacts and becomes very belligerent or runs away. He or she may express hatred of homosexuality and be totally unaware that this excessive response reflects a wish to deny his or her own feelings.

Before homosexuality was as acceptable as it is today—and it is still not widely acceptable—psychiatrists would see patients with "homosexual panic." These were persons with no awareness of their repressed latent homosexual feelings. An experience such as a sexual overture by a homosexual would make them conscious of their own feelings and they would become overwhelmed by guilt. They would be so disturbed that they would jump out of a window or attempt suicide. They were among the most agitated patients seen in a psychiatric hospital.

A number of individuals still come to the psychiatrist's office terrified that they will find out they have homosexual feelings. This concern emphasizes one of the basic themes of this chapter: *Having the feelings does not mean one must act on them*. We all have homosexual feelings. The important questions are (see Madow 1982, Chapter 6):

- Where do the feelings come from?
- How guilty do we feel about them?
- Where does the guilt come from?
- How much do these feelings interfere with living a happy life?
- What do we do with these feelings?

FRED

An example of a problem with latent homosexuality was seen in Fred, a 36-year-old dentist, who came to therapy because he was depressed, anxious, and having difficulty concentrating on his work. He was married and had one son, aged 4. His marriage was floundering. He feared his wife would leave him. The difficulties began when his wife found out that he was having extramarital affairs. As the history unfolded, Fred indicated that he felt he had to seduce every woman he met. Because many of his patients were women, there were frequent opportunities. His wife found out about one of these affairs and, in turn, began having extramarital relations, too. Fred said that he couldn't understand why he had this drive to seduce all of these women because he actually did not enjoy the sexual experience itself that much [see Don Juan Syndrome, Fenichel (1944)]. The real pleasure was in the challenge. Once he got the woman into bed, the sex itself was usually not that gratifying. It was clear that Fred's greatest satisfaction was in the conquest.

When he first came to see me, Fred believed he had an excessive sex drive and simply needed a great deal more sex than most men. His history revealed that his mother and father were not close. The father held two jobs and was rarely at home. A passive, quiet man, he lived for his work and took little interest in his wife or son. The mother, on the other hand, doted on Fred, spending most of her time with him, since the father showed her no affection on the rare times he was home. Fred was afraid of his father and hated him because he did nothing for the family except provide money. Fred felt guilty and frightened about his close relationship with his mother, especially since his father did caution him not to become a "Momma's boy." Fred, therefore, found himself trying to please and placate his father as well as other men he met in order to show them how manly he was. He worked hard to become a good athlete, which was the one thing he could do to please his father.

Fred had unconscious homosexual feelings that arose out of an effort to deal with the guilt feelings he felt about his mother, in addition to the fear of his father and the desire to please him. He was unaware of these feelings and attempted to deny their existence by becoming excessively active heterosexually.

When Fred was able to understand and accept his real feelings and where they came from, he was able to deal with them realistically.

Parents often experience a great deal of guilt when they learn that their child is a homosexual. This reaction frequently follows the grieving stages seen in parents of any handicapped child. At first they attempt to deny the fact. Then they become enraged, and this is followed by feelings of guilt that may overwhelm them.

LEONARD

Leonard came to see me because of his depression on learning that his daughter Sara was homosexual. Sara was 32 years old and living with her friend Joanne. She had isolated herself from her parents for two years and when she finally communicated with them, revealed that she had a child by a male homosexual friend who had "accommodated" her.

Leonard was stunned. He had been reared by a strict, Protestant family in a small town near Cleveland and had very narrow sexual standards. At first he refused to accept Sara's sexual orientation, saying this was only a phase growing out of Sara's Greenwich Village days and that she would outgrow it. When Sara persisted and made it clear that this was her chosen lifestyle, he became furious and told his wife that they should disown her. Sara wanted to continue the relationship with her parents, and soon they became attached to her baby boy (their grandchild). Leonard then repressed his anger and began feeling guilty, fearing that he had done something early in her life to turn Sara against men. The persistent repressed anger and excessive guilt led to his depression.

Both emotions had to be recognized and explored in order to alleviate his feelings of depression.

Sexual Offenders

A full description of sexual offenders would require another volume. Some have antisocial personality disorders and may have no remorse about their behavior, only resentment at being caught. Others have great guilt about their acts, hoping to be caught so that they *can* be stopped and punished, leaving clues and messages saying "Catch me before I do it again." They may, indeed, be performing the acts out of guilt about their sexual feelings, in the hope of being apprehended. Rage may be an important component in the act for the offender, the chief interest being to express violent rather than sexual feelings.

Despite the efforts of active groups to diminish the psychological and emotional trauma, there are still women who feel guilty if they have been raped. This may be due in part to the fact that the men in their lives may directly or indirectly accuse them of having invited the act. The men who do this have their own problems, often feeling insecure about their own manliness.

The important question is why any woman would even consider accepting the blame to explore her own thoughts and actions to see if she really instigated the rape!

One possibility is that it is not uncommon for women to have rape fantasies arising from a wish that the sexual act be outside control and, therefore, not their own responsibility. Another aspect of forced sex is the pleasure some women derive from being dominated. These are not acceptable wishes; they are repressed and out of the woman's awareness. If she is raped, the experience may stir up the denied fantasy. The woman develops guilt feelings because the unacceptable fantasy has now been fulfilled.

Although their numbers are decreasing, there are still a significant number of women who have sex with their husbands as a "wifely duty" or for procreation and rarely, if ever, enjoy it as a purely pleasurable act. They may feel guilty if they do enjoy it. Some religions still teach that one *must not enjoy sex,* but that it should be used only for procreation. This decree may become self-fulfilling, the fear making it impossible to respond. Some women are also influenced by parental attitudes that sex is "dirty" and only loose women enjoy it.

On the other side, there are men who enjoy sex with a prostitute much more than with their wives. There are some men who can have sex only with harlots.

CASEY

Casey said he had a problem with women. Whenever he met a nice Irish girl to whom he was attracted, something always seemed to come up, and they would separate. If the woman tried to get sexually involved, Casey would become anxious and have to leave.

Casey was the only son of a doting Irish mother. He could do no wrong in her eyes, and he was devoted to her. His father spent most of his time away from home, either at work or drinking. Casey was clearly his mother's chief love.

When Casey was 15, one of the girls in his class showed affection for him, but when they began kissing and petting, Casey panicked and ran away. Shortly thereafter, one of his friends took him to a house of prostitution and he chose a black woman with whom he said he enjoyed the sex very much. Thereafter he sought out sex with prostitutes but could not get close to what he called "nice white women." As he talked about it, it was evident Casey worshiped his mother, saw her as a Madonna, not to be dirtied by sex. These "nice white women" reminded him of his mother, and sex was forbidden with them. The black prostitute was acceptable as a sex object, so that Casey was able to enjoy intercourse with her.

Casey needed to work on his confusion, feeling that all "nice white women" were like his mother. He had to see them as individuals with their own personalities and characteristics.

Pregnancy

Guilt over pregnancy out of wedlock is decreasing, but it is present in many cases. Statistics reveal that in 1960 in the United States, 5 percent of unmarried women had children. By 1982, it had increased to 19.4 percent (*Vital Statistics,* 1982). As an example, in that same year, the Associated Press reported that 75 percent of babies born to women 19 years old and younger in the State of New Jersey were born to unwed mothers. Over 21 percent of all babies born in that state in that year were also born out of wedlock. In thirteen cities in New Jersey the number of births out of wedlock outnumbered children born to married couples.

Alta Garfield, head of the Family Planning Units of the New Jersey Health Department, said, "I don't know how you can stop this. We are doing all we can to change it, but society doesn't really frown on the unwed mother anymore. The attitude is, 'so the kid got pregnant.' "

Perhaps society needs more healthy guilt!

Abortion is a topic that has not only religious, legal, and social implications but it is also a powerful guilt producer as well. Depending upon one's religious beliefs, a woman can feel so guilty about having an abortion that she will go through with the pregnancy and insist on rearing the child, sacrificing her future to do so. If she does have the abortion, her guilt feelings may hound her for the rest of her life. The "right to life" groups are adding to the guilt feelings women have about abortion. There are now legal efforts being made to protect the rights of the unborn child, battling against the woman's right to control her own body.

There are no simple answers. Abortion is a complex issue. It involves better education regarding birth control, religious attitudes, and women's rights. If the guilt is excessive, the reasons need to be explored and dealt with as indicated in the last chapter of this book.

There are now women who prefer to have their own children outside of marriage and clearly have no guilt about the sex act itself. There are many reasons for this. The lack of guilt may be related to the old attitude that one should not enjoy sex but having sex for procreational purposes is acceptable. It may have to do with the feelings these women have about men. There may be the implied statement that, with artificial insemination, men are not even needed for procreation, and women can get pregnant themselves. Women feel more equal to men than ever before. Having children outside of marriage may be a way of asserting one's independence and of avoiding a close relationship.

The other side of the coin, and a painful generator of guilt, is *infertility*. Women who are unable to conceive often develop intense guilt feelings over their inability to become pregnant. Each month when they begin to menstruate and they realize they are not pregnant, they feel tremendous guilt, and often rage at themselves. If the man is the source of the infertility, he, too, may feel it is a reflection of his manhood and blame himself. Both may develop anger and express it against the spouse, placing the blame on the other as the source of the problem. If they blame themselves, they may become depressed.

Infertility is still considered a reason for dissolving a marriage in some religions, adding fear to the guilt feelings of the victim. What must be recognized is that infertility may be a physiological, an anatomical, or a psychological problem for which no one is responsible. If it is hormonal or due to some physical abnormality, that problem needs to be corrected. If it is psychological, professional help may be needed. Blaming oneself or feeling guilty not only does not resolve the problem but also adds to the emotional stress.

There are many fears that may interfere with impregnation, fears of which the woman may often not be aware. These include (among many others) fear of pregnancy itself, fear of the effects of the pregnancy on the woman's body, fear of death as a result of the pregnancy, fear of having a defective child, and fear of the responsibility of rearing a child. The woman may not be conscious of her fears and be plagued with guilt feelings. These, unfortunately, may be reinforced by her doctor who tells her there is "nothing wrong" with her, adding to her guilt. The statement "There is nothing wrong" is misleading. There may be no anatomical or physical reason for problems relating to conception, but there *is* something wrong. Emotional reasons can interfere with a successful pregnancy as much as an obstructed Fallopian tube.

Impotence in men may also be a contributor to guilt feelings. There are physical reasons for impotence in some men including anatomical abnormalities, diabetes, and the use of certain medications. These must be ruled out. If no organic problem is found, however, the impotent man may feel extreme guilt. It may mean to him that he is not a man. If he attempts intercourse and is unable to perform, it becomes a self-fulfilling prophecy. Each time he tries he is so concerned and preoccupied that he is again impotent. Some men become so fearful of the impotence that they withdraw from women totally.

Psychological impotence is treatable and can be reversed in many cases. There is no reason to feel guilty about it.

As people get older, they often believe that they are not supposed to have any interest in sex, and they feel dirty and guilty if they continue to have sexual desires. This reaction may be reinforced by their offspring because of their feelings about parents' sexual activities.

A man had arranged for his mother, a widow, to live in one of the modern senior citizens' complexes in which each person has his or her own apartment and is independent. Residents took their evening meals together, and this provided an excellent opportunity for companionship and avoided the need for cooking for oneself. Medical care was also available. The mother adapted well to her new surroundings, but told the following story:

One member of the community was an 88-year-old man who was beginning to fail physically. He was unable to dress and bathe himself and required a nurse to care for him. She usually went home at night, but one evening there was a severe snowstorm, and the nurse decided to sleep overnight in the old man's apartment. The next morning when the other residents, including my friend's mother, learned that the nurse had stayed overnight, they were scandalized. The situation had brought shame and disgrace to the establishment! A number of women felt the man should be evicted.

Perhaps we should not overlook their optimism that something may indeed have taken place! Disapproval of sex in the elderly comes not only from the young!

Concern and guilt about sex is felt throughout our life, from infancy and early childhood when we first enjoyed stimulating ourselves to old age, as with senior citizens in nursing homes who are considered to be perverted if they show any interest in sex.

The freeing up of the constricted attitude toward sex in our society is decreasing the guilt generated. There remain taboos, however, that cause shame and guilt about sexual desires. Many religions still adhere to their prohibitions about various sexual activities. A number of states maintain laws forbidding certain sexual practices such as adultery or homosexuality. The important thing to remember is that the sexual drive is present in all of us. We must accept the fact that we have such interests and not feel guilty about having the feelings. This does not mean we must always act on these urges directly. Seeing a woman in the street who is sexually desirable does not justify raping her. The woman who is attracted to her friend's husband does not necessarily have the right to seduce him. She can acknowledge to herself that he is desirable and need not feel guilty about *having* those feelings, as long as she does not act on them *and* accepts comfortably that he belongs to her friend. A healthy conscience and healthy guilt will stop us from acting out these sexual feelings when they are inappropriate or harmful to others and, ultimately, to ourselves.

It is the unhealthy, excessive guilt about sex that interferes with one of the great pleasures in our lives.

4

Guilt and Anger

Sexual desires are well recognized as a major source of guilt feelings. Although not as well known, an equally important source of guilt is one's own hostility and anger. These "destructive" feelings come from two chief sources.

Even though moral codes and conscience develop, *the aggressive instinct and its wishes persist*. We become more and more aware that it is not acceptable or even safe to wish to destroy things and/or people. These instinctual wishes frighten us. We develop guilt and try to deny them. As a child, after all, one lives in a world of giants. We recognize early that we are physically smaller than our parents and feel helpless against their superior physiques. We sense that they could indeed crush us if they so desired.

Fear is converted to guilt as our conscience develops, and we feel guilty if we only become aware of wishes to harm someone. Yet if an unfortunate person is standing on a ledge of a high building threatening to kill himself, how often do people in the watching crowd yell, "Jump, Jump!" That is about as aggressive as one can get.

Another and even greater source of guilt over negative feelings comes from acquired anger. All of us have anger, much of which we may be aware of, but a large part of which may be unconscious. Where does all this anger come from? A normal part of the process of growing up is frustration, and frustration leads to anger (see Madow 1972). But we are constantly being taught we must love our parents, our neighbors, and our friends, and not be angry with them. If we have feelings of anger toward them, we feel guilty because it is wrong, and therefore, must be bad.

SAM

Sam was a painful example of the relationship between guilt and anger. He came to see me because he was depressed and had multiple somatic complaints. Sam was a 66-year-old retired engineer who had looked forward to his retirement when he would be free to travel, take courses in philosophy, and go to shows and concerts that he had been unable to attend while he was working his 60-hour week as a consulting engineer.

Unfortunately, a year before he retired, his wife began showing signs of forgetfulness and temper outbursts. In place of the bright, alert woman he had known, she was now unable to remember her grocery list or keep her own bank account. She had always been an independent, capable woman but was now becoming increasingly dependent on her husband and fearful of being left alone. The doctor made a diagnosis of Alzheimer's disease and told Sam the prognosis was poor.

Instead of being able to get out and do all the things he had been dreaming of, Sam was now essentially confined to the house. Every time he did go out, leaving his wife alone, he felt tremendous guilt as well as fear that something would happen to her. Upon his return home from a morning visit to the local museum, he was consumed with guilt because his wife was upset at his being away and had upbraided him for leaving her.

He described a typical experience when he visited with an old friend and the man insisted that they go to lunch. He returned home around 2:30 P.M. His wife had not eaten and was waiting for him. His guilt was enormous. He felt that he was being neglectful and mean to her. He lived in constant fear whenever he left her that she would become agitated and might harm herself.

As she became more disabled, he struggled with his conflicting feelings but refused to place her in a nursing home.

"I've thought about it," he said, "but I just can't bring myself to do it. I could not stand my guilt."

Beneath all of this, of course, was his intense resentment of the burden of her care at a time when he had planned to begin enjoying life, but his guilt made him deny his frustration and disappointment.

Sam made attempts to solve their problems in a rational manner. He hired daytime nurses. His wife complained about them. If he left the house, she would remain in bed until he returned, refusing to do anything the nurses asked. When Sam was at home, he would encourage her to be active and urged her to use her mind more. Again he would be overwhelmed with guilt, wondering whether or not he was pushing her beyond her capabilities or whether she really did need his support and his gentle but firm insistence that she do things in order to stimulate her to be more active. He did have a son and daughter, but he felt he had no right to impose the burden of his wife's care on them.

Occasionally, when he would become infuriated with her carelessness and "lack of cooperation," he would explode at her. This would be followed by overwhelming feelings of guilt. He believed that he had no right to be angry with his sick, unfortunate wife and that she was unable to do more than she did.

What was the basic problem? Sam cared for and felt genuinely sorry for his wife, recognizing how incapacitated she was, but he was also struggling with his private rage. He felt he had no right to be angry because his wife did not become ill deliberately and was suffering along with him. He, therefore, felt overwhelmingly guilty about anything he did that could possibly be construed as an expression of his anger. In bending over backwards to deny his frustration, he was refusing to accept the reality of his wife's disability. He felt that she would do much better if he was with her all the time, which was true only within the limits of her disability. Early in her illness she would watch television with him, but as the disease progressed, she would wander off. Sam continued to feel that he should be home to entertain her even though she could no longer respond.

Sam's marriage had not been a particularly gratifying one. He had always felt that his wife was self-centered and preferred having a good time to taking care of the home and family. He loved his wife but believed that no marriage was perfect. He had looked forward to retirement, to a time when he might be able to indulge himself as she had done.

When Sam came to see me, he was having difficulty sleeping, and he had no appetite. He said that he was not sure that life was worth living. At his annual physical checkup, he had been told that his blood pressure was somewhat elevated. Although an x-ray of his stomach revealed no ulcer, he was having pains before meals and taking antacids. He had been given Valium to get to sleep at night but was afraid to take it, concerned that he might sleep through the night and not hear his wife if she needed him.

During the course of treatment, he was able to express his great anger and resentment at his situation. He became aware that his guilt feelings were generated by these resentments.

One time he blurted out, "I wish she were dead!"

He was immediately overwhelmed by guilt and quickly apologized, "How can I even think such a thing! This is not her fault."

Eventually, he came to accept that the best care for his wife was in a good nursing home. Although his visits to her were frequent, they were often painful because she would yell at him for not visiting her often enough. As her forgetfulness increased, she would not remember that he had been to see her the day before and would scold him for not having been to see her for months. With time, he was able to see that she actually was quite comfortable and getting better nursing care than he could provide at home.

Sam's background had, unfortunately, paved the way for his reactions and laid the groundwork for his excessive guilt feelings. He had been reared by a devoted mother who, however, demanded that he be attentive to her. When he went away to college, she insisted that he call her twice a week. If he did not, she would make him feel guilty. His father had died when Sam was 22 years old. His mother made it clear that she was living only for him and, therefore, made him feel totally responsible for her. When she was 70 years old, she had a mild left-sided stroke to which she reacted by insisting that she was entirely helpless. She demanded that he take her shopping and help her with her various errands, despite the fact that he was married and had a child. His mother expected her needs to come first. Sam would suffer tremendous guilt if he did not comply with her wishes. When Sam's wife became ill, it stirred up not only the guilt feelings he had about neglecting her but also reawakened all of the guilt feelings he had had about his mother when he did not cater to her demands. The rage against his wife that he repressed was added to the anger he had accumulated and denied against his mother.

When unreasonable demands are made upon us, we are usually comfortable with our resentment of them and feel relatively little guilt about the anger. In situations such as Sam found himself, however, where the needs of our loved ones arise through no fault of their own (illness or accident), and we cannot in good conscience blame them for it, we often feel compelled to deny any anger or resentment and feel guilty if such emotions are revealed. Sam felt inadequate because his wife was suffering pain and discomfort, and he was unable to make her feel better. His wife was frightened and furious about being ill, and she often accused him of not doing enough for her, just as his mother did. Unfortunately, since such duties kept him from doing what *he* wanted to do, he resented the demands. His rage at these two important women in his life was unacceptable to him, and it generated guilt feelings, forcing him to deny his anger. It was not until Sam could recognize his anger and realize that it was normal, regardless of its not being logical or reasonable (emotions are not always logical), that he was relieved of his guilt and could deal with the situation as required.

Another important connection between anger and guilt exists when we are furious with the people who make us feel guilty.

A man becomes enraged with his wife when she tells him he is drinking too much. The anger comes from her making him feel guilty about his overindulging, which he knows is true. Another man strikes his wife when she accuses him of having an affair. He has been flirting with a young woman in his office. His wife's confrontation stirs his guilt feelings, leading to anger. Often we develop guilt about our anger, thus compounding the guilt feelings.

Why do we get angry with someone who makes us feel guilty? Usually, it is because we feel there is some truth in the observation.

A mother with a drinking problem had an adolescent son who was in difficulty with drugs, using marijuana and occasionally cocaine. When she tried to discipline him, he said, "You can't tell me what to do! Look how you drink, and you don't control yourself!"

She became furious with her son and attempted to strike him, not realizing that she was angry with him because he made her feel guilty about her own drinking. Her son had made an accurate observation that she had not wanted to face. She felt guilty when he pointed it out and was furious with him for doing so.

We may get angry when someone accuses us unjustly, with no basis for the accusation, but we do not usually feel guilty about the anger.

PETER

Peter was a 34-year-old divorced accountant who came to see me because he was worried about thoughts of suicide. He believed it was all due to his failure as a husband and a father. Peter had met his future wife in a bar, began dating her, and they soon developed a serious relationship. She was married at the time, but after meeting Peter she divorced her husband and they were married. The marriage was stormy from the start, with frequent fights over what Peter, at first, characterized as trivial things. He had struck her on several occasions. Now he realized that he had mistreated her and indicated that he really cared for her. They had two daughters whom Peter loved very much. Unfortunately, the fights with his wife became violent, more frequent, and eventually led to divorce. Although Peter indicated that his wife had begun having an affair with another man, he believed that he had driven her to it because that is what she told him.

Following the divorce, Peter made every effort to spend as much time as possible with the two girls. However, his ex-wife had sent him a letter accusing him of not being a good father and informing him that their daughters were having behavioral and performance difficulties in school because of him. Peter felt guilty about this and accepted the blame, feeling that he had not paid enough attention to them and that the problem was all his fault.

He began smoking and drinking excessively and came to see me because he said he was having thoughts of suicide.

As his story unfolded, it became clear that he was furious with his wife for the way she treated him, but he denied his anger and blamed himself for her actions. He carried guilt about the failure of the marriage. His wife had repeated the pattern of her first marriage during which she had had a number of affairs. Now, she had begun living openly with her most recent lover while still married to Peter. Peter minimized that situation at first and was preoccupied with his guilt feelings over his neglect of the family.

When he was able to accept his anger toward his wife and could be more reasonable about not blaming himself totally for his daughters' problems, he then could deal with his daughters more productively. His depression lifted.

Peter's wife had been skillful in making him feel guilty about his actions, which further enraged him, but he was unable to accept his own anger and felt even more guilty about it. He had attempted to deny the rage and turned it inward. This led to his depression and suicidal thoughts.

STELLA

An example of anger generating guilt that seemed unwarranted and came as a surprise was related by Stella, a successful department store executive. She was a 46-year-old woman who came to see me because she was feeling depressed. She said that she was married to a man who had become withdrawn and had not worked for twenty years.

"He sits around the house all day and mopes and drinks," she complained, adding, "I'm disgusted with him!"

In her twenty-five years of marriage she had had numerous affairs, mostly short-lived ones, because she was seeking companionship and affection and her lovers soon revealed that they were only interested in sex. Recently, Stella had met a married man who seemed genuinely interested in her. She was certain that he was not just seeking a physical relationship. She felt she loved him, but he had begun to change and was not as interested in the serious relationship she had desired.

I asked her how she would like to change, expecting her to say that she wanted to handle this association with the man more reasonably, particularly dealing with her disappointment and anger over his beginning to withdraw from her.

She said, "My main problem is my guilt." When I asked her to elaborate, she said, "I feel terribly guilty toward my husband for having this affair, and I would like to get rid of the guilt."

There was complete denial of her rage toward her husband and her lover, both of whom were disappointing her. Her inability to cope with her anger toward her husband made her deny the rage, and then she felt guilty, unconsciously, for having such feelings. The guilt was then transferred to the relationship with the married man. Consciously she really wanted to get rid of the guilt feelings she had regarding her husband.

Could the real guilt have come from her desire to get rid of her husband, a wish that was totally unacceptable to her? She described outbursts of fury at her spouse for his repeated episodes of depression and his inability to hold a job. Then she developed tremendous guilt over her outbursts.

She said, "He's really a good man. He has never been mean to me. He can't help it if he can't hold a job or gets depressed. He drinks so much because he feels he is a failure. When he is normal, he is the nicest man you would ever want to meet."

Contrast Stella with Peter's wife, who had no guilt feelings about her affair and blamed Peter for everything.

Anger is not necessarily directed toward a person. There are some people who become furious with their church for imposing guilt on them, and they leave the church. I have seen a number of patients, many of them Catholics reared in strict religious homes, who attended parochial school and at adolescence (a period of rebellion) turned against the church, which they regarded as the source of their suffering.

RANDY

Randy, an intelligent, busy building contractor came to see me because he had become depressed following his separation from his wife. He had been reared in a strict Catholic home, had attended parochial school and a Catholic college. He married an attractive fellow student who was also an observant Catholic. His wife resented the increasing amounts of time he needed to spend away from home in order to develop his business. She accused him of neglecting her and made him feel guilty. She would harangue him until he was acutely anxious and provoked to the point that he would hit her. I asked him where his guilt feelings came from.

He said, "It's my Catholic upbringing, particularly the Ten Commandments."

I asked him, "Which one in particular?"

He said, "Thou shalt not kill."

He did not feel he could divorce his wife because of his religious beliefs. She continued to accuse him of neglecting the family and of being selfish. He told of one incident that occurred following a cocktail party where he circulated among his friends. On the way home, she accused him of not paying attention to her. A vicious argument ensued. He slapped her and then felt intense guilt.

Randy enjoyed going to baseball games. Whenever he did, his wife accused him of not spending enough time with her. These accusations infuriated him.

They did not practice birth control because of their religious beliefs and now had six children, creating pressure on him to support them in the manner he felt he should. He was enraged when his wife used partial truths, such as his being away from home, to accuse him of neglecting the children, but he accepted these accusations and felt guilty.

He described his anger at the church for creating all the guilt in him. He had left the church about five years ago but felt guilty when his wife accused him of setting a poor example for the children.

In the course of treatment Randy was able to recognize how much he had denied the resentment he felt about his wife's charges. Though he said he was no longer religious, he could not bring himself to seek a divorce. He would continue to go to church with his children occasionally, out of a sense of obligation toward the children and under the continued harassment of his wife.

As mentioned, guilt can generate anger toward the creator of the guilt. Anger, in turn, can stir up guilt over having this unacceptable emotion. When guilt stirs angry feelings in us, we can handle the anger in several ways. We can turn it outward against the person or thing that makes us feel angry, as in the example of the husband who hit his wife after she accused him of being unfaithful. His conscience knew it was true, but her accusation infuriated him. We can get angry at a policeman who gives us a ticket even when it is deserved, and get into an argument with him, which usually results in even more problems.

Expressing anger outward may in itself generate strong feelings of guilt. Robert's wife had had a heart attack recently, and he had been cautioned not to expose her to any undue stress. One day when he was taking his wife for a ride, she began backseat driving, criticizing him for not stopping completely at a stop sign. He flared up in anger at her but immediately felt guilty and feared that he might have precipitated another heart attack. The irrational part of his anger, and one that provokes guilt, is that he probably wished that his invalid wife would disappear because she had become a burden to him, a wish he had completely repressed.

Illness frequently generates anger in the sick person, who then becomes irritable and expresses it toward caretakers and loved ones, who are then caught in a bind. They are angry over the demands of the disabled person and find themselves the object of increased anger. The anger is often not acceptable because the poor individual is, after all, sick and suffering, and the healthy spouse, son or daughter may deny it.

Another effort to deal with our anger and the guilt over having such feelings is to turn it against ourselves and actually seek punishment for the guilt feelings from others or attempt to punish ourselves. Punishment for having done something about which we feel guilty frequently alleviates the feelings, at least temporarily.

Children who feel guilty are often relieved when punished and then forget the incident. The punishment need not be physical, but the child should be made aware of the parent's disapproval of the unacceptable act. A too-understanding parent sometimes prolongs the pain and suffering of the guilt or may confuse the child. As an adult we may say to another person whom we have wronged, "Why don't you yell at me and get it over with!" We are trying to relieve our guilt feelings by seeking punishment and thus hope to conclude the episode. It may also satisfy the hurt of the wronged person by allowing that person to express his or her anger.

To say "I was hurt, but let's forget it!" when the guilty person knows it will not be forgotten prolongs the guilty feelings, and that may be the unconscious intention of the offended person.

We are familiar with the overly attached mother who feels that she has been neglected by her offspring. She says, "Don't you worry about me. I know how busy you are. I'll get along— somehow!"

She is attempting to increase the guilt feelings in the son or daughter, thus expressing her hostility. The literal words sound conciliatory, but the intention is clear.

SEYMOUR

Seymour was referred to me because he had repeated episodes of chest pain and lived in dread of a heart attack. He was a 36-year-old traveling salesman who knew the location of every hospital on his route in several cities. He was also well known to the doctors in the emergency rooms. Each time he developed what he called his "heart pains," he was certain he was dying of cardiac failure and would rush to the nearest emergency room where he would be told he had tachycardia (rapid heartbeats) or palpitations but that his heart was in good shape. Occasionally, he would be hospitalized by a conservative doctor.

These hospitalizations would often add to his anxiety, especially if the doctor would say, "Well, everything seems to check out, but you'd better let me see you in a month."

Seymour would panic and rush home to his family doctor who would reassure him. Such reassurance would not last, however, and when the chest pains recurred, off he would go to another emergency room.

Seymour was an adopted child. His adoptive father was a successful businessman who was not home much, and Seymour's mother devoted herself to caring for him. When he finally broke away from home and married, he expected his wife to continue the overindulgent mothering role.

He selected Sadie because she was maternal, but Seymour felt she never did enough for him. Whenever she asked for money for household expenses, he would become furious, realize the irrationality of his anger, feel guilty, and repress the rage. If she showed an interest in sex, he would usually be impotent, secretly enraged that she would make this demand on him, but he felt guilty about not being able to satisfy her and repressed his angry feelings. In truth, he was only interested in having her satisfy him sexually by manual manipulation. As the repressed anger accumulated, he developed the chest pains.

When I first saw Seymour, he focused on what a failure he was as a husband and how guilty he felt about it. The chest pains were interfering with his ability to earn a living, and his mother was contributing to the family's support. Notice how his symptoms brought his mother into his life to perpetuate her mothering role. He even used the fear of a heart attack to avoid sexual contact with his wife.

As treatment progressed, it became clear that Seymour was furious with his wife for not continuing the indulgent mothering to which he was accustomed. He came to realize the anger was not justified and felt guilty about having such unreasonable feelings. Unconsciously, he felt that if he expressed the anger, he might lose his wife, who, indeed, tried to cater to his wishes. To handle the anger and relieve his guilt, he turned it against himself and tormented himself with the constant threat of heart failure and death. As his anger and guilt feelings were revealed, he was able to accept that they existed but recognized the need to understand where they came from. He was able to deal with them by recognizing that his wife was not his mother and that, moreover, he no longer needed all the mothering that had been such an important part of his life.

One of the more common sources of guilt is the fear that we may have offended someone and that that person will become angry with us. We may worry, review the incident again and again, and become preoccupied with guilt. Even if the action or remark did displease, the reaction is excessive.

Andy's car battery was dead. He walked to a nearby gas station to ask for a jump start. The attendant said he was all alone but there was a number he could call and that mechanic would help. He phoned the man who said he was some distance away but would come. As Andy walked back to his car, he encountered a man who said he would get him started. Andy was impatient to get home, accepted the offer, then asked the man to give the mechanic who was on his way five dollars for his trouble. The man agreed, but Andy worried all the way home that he had offended the mechanic and he would be angry. He tormented himself with his guilt. Why did he ever call him? He should have looked around and he would have found the Good Samaritan. What if the man didn't give the mechanic the money? Why didn't I just wait for him? Andy was unable to sleep that night, thought about going back to the gas station, getting the mechanic's number, apologizing and giving him more money. Andy had much more guilt than the situation warranted.

Generally, when we worry excessively about displeasing someone, our excessive anger has revealed itself, usually an anger of which we had not been aware. Andy was frustrated that his battery was dead and that he had to wait an hour for someone to help him. He had tried to deny those feelings and rationalized that car batteries do go dead, and the mechanic was not just sitting at home waiting for him. Leaving without waiting for the mechanic was not thoughtful and exposed Andy's repressed anger. He could not accept his hostile action and tormented himself with guilt. This type of guilt not only punished him but it also interfered with his thinking clearly and resolving the issue reasonably.

Our angry and destructive wishes, which may seem irrational to us, are a major source of guilt. We must accept the fact that these wishes do exist and that we are not monsters for having them. We cannot deal with them realistically until we recognize their existence (see Madow 1972).

5

Narcissistic Guilt

When we speak of guilt, we are usually referring to the reaction to having done something wrong for which we will or should be punished. This is the classical form of guilt arising from a feeling that we have violated our own standards.

There is also a specific form of self-blame, in which the concern is not only that we have done something wrong, but also that the action is one that will lead to our humiliation, embarrassment, or make us look foolish. It is a feeling that we have harmed or belittled our self-image.

Although a number of authorities call this reaction shame, and this will be discussed later in this chapter, it is so often combined with guilt that I believe it is more useful to call it narcissistic guilt.

The term narcissism as used here refers to a concentration of emotional interest in oneself. It is self-love and in its healthy form pertains to self-esteem, self-confidence, and a realistic self-image. Under normal circumstances our love is divided between ourselves (narcissism) and the outside world (object love). Both are important for a healthy personality. Unfortunately, the term is often misused to describe excessive narcissism where the person thinks only of himself and has not developed sufficient object love.

A narcissistic injury occurs when an experience leads to belittlement, embarrassment, or ridicule.

In narcissistic guilt the focus is on the feeling that one has done something wrong that does little if any harm to someone else but that reflects badly on oneself. The narcissistic injury is self-inflicted and stirs up anger at oneself and guilt feelings for having done so.

This guilt may result from a wide range of activities. One person may feel guilty for having stepped on his partner's foot while dancing and privately suffers for having been clumsy and appearing awkward. Another man has a few drinks at a party and kisses his best male friend. He is then tormented, feeling guilty for having done "such a thing," concerned that everyone will think he is a homosexual, and worried he may be a sexual pervert. He feels he did a terrible thing, he may have harmed his friend, and he feels guilt.

A 45-year-old man in analysis, a successful judge, described the following experience:

> *It was in the third grade. I passed a note to a girl I liked. My teacher called me on it. I felt so embarrassed. I was enraged, furious with myself for having done it. I felt guilty; the teacher made it look like I had done a terrible thing, and I hated myself for having put myself in this position. I knew I had done something wrong, but I did it to myself.*

He suffered a self-inflicted narcissistic mortification and felt shamed by the teacher. But, she also made him feel he had done something terribly wrong and he experienced intense, persistent guilt.

There are many other types of behavior that may make us feel guilty because they lead to a narcissistic wound, making us feel demeaned or disgraced. Our reactions to the guilt feelings can sometimes lead to extreme measures.

PHIL

Phil was reserved and shy to the point of speaking with a hesitation, not quite a stutter or stammer. His face was rugged, but when he smiled, his eyes twinkled. He said that he was lonely, having retired the year before from his job as a bookkeeper for a sweater manufacturer. Paradoxically he indicated that he enjoyed being by himself to pursue his hobbies of gardening and reading. He did feel somewhat depressed, however, and was particularly concerned about the weekends when he would frequent bars, hoping to meet women but too shy to make any overtures. He knew he was drinking too much and was concerned that it might be affecting his health.

Phil's wife had died three years ago. With some feeling, he described the marriage as an unhappy one. His round, English face broke into a smile when he added, "I sure don't miss her!"

He had been reared in a blue-collar ghetto, and his father and mother were both heavy drinkers. His father was a laborer in the local steel mill. His main interest was the corner saloon where he spent his evenings. He remembered almost daily fights between his father and mother when she would scream, "Stay away from me!"

Phil would withdraw to his room and read. He was extremely shy with women and a loner. He was driven to educate himself, working his way both through college and business school, eventually obtaining a position that he enjoyed. He was mostly alone; his account books were his friends and challenge.

He said that he enjoyed women and thought a great deal about sex; but he was sensitive about it and found it painful to approach a woman. The only sexual experience he had had before marriage was with a girl who was known as the "nympho" in his class. He said, "The minute you walked into her house, she had her clothes off and practically attacked you!"

As a result of his shyness, Phil had few dates and turned to his reading. He developed an interest in wood carving and had made over a hundred pieces, although he had not yet produced anything that satisfied him.

He met his wife while he was a senior in college. She was already drinking heavily, one of the things they had in common. There was one couple with whom they would usually spend the weekends drinking.

As he was telling this story, he looked me in the eye with a searching look and said slowly and with great apprehension, "I'm going to tell you something now, Doctor, that I never told anyone in my life.

"One weekend, the four of us were together drinking as usual in their living room, joking and laughing, when suddenly I farted. I was so embarrassed and shocked I ran out of the room into the kitchen. I felt guilty and tried to hide.

"My friend came in after me and said, 'Look, that was nothing at all!' He tried to make light of it. I was too embarrassed to go back into the living room, but he jollied me into returning.

"As we continued drinking, his girlfriend commented, 'You know, I couldn't do that in front of Joe here until we had been going together for two years!' She told this with much laughter and amusement.

"My girlfriend also seemed to pass it off, but I could not overcome my embarrassment and humiliation.

"You are not going to believe this, Doctor, but I felt so guilty about embarrassing my girl in front of our friends that I felt I had to marry her, and I did. I was so ashamed. It was a miserable thirty years. She was obviously not the woman for me, and yet I felt responsible and had such guilt over having done that in front of our friends that I felt I had no choice but to marry her."

Phil spoke interchangeably of feeling guilty and ashamed. It is interesting to note that the others were not offended by what Phil did. In fact, they were amused by it. Phil, however, felt that his social transgression had humiliated and embarrassed him and his girl and that he was obligated to right the wrong he had committed against her.

Some psychoanalysts (Piers and Singer, Wurmser, Lewis) would call this reaction shame. They believe that guilt and shame arise from different sources and, therefore, need to be dealt with differently. It is helpful to understand the distinction because it makes a difference in how one deals with the problems that arise. Shame is usually an emotion we feel when we have not attained goals that were established for us or that we have set up for ourselves.

As described in Chapter 2, there is a part of our personality that has special high goals and standards we would like to live by.

It is called the ego ideal. This is different from the conscience or superego. We react to our superego when we believe we have done something wrong. Our conscience or superego actually develops differently and plays a different role in our lives than does the ego ideal. It is when we do something to transgress our superego that we feel guilty. An example: If we cheat someone and feel that we did wrong, then we feel guilty. The man who has an extramarital affair and feels that he did something wrong feels guilty. We tend to confuse shame with embarrassment, frequently saying "I was ashamed of having my bathing suit slip down on the beach," when we really mean we felt embarrassed. The source of embarrassment comes from yet another part of our personality, our ego.

Embarrassment is usually related to the revelation of a hidden forbidden wish such as the wish to exhibit ourselves, or the wish to tell a dirty story, or to appear very sexual. Embarrassment is a response by the ego, which is resisting the id impulses, usually to some sexual drive ranging from narcissistic desires, oral wishes, wishes to exhibit oneself, or genital sexual fantasies. One of the most painful of all emotional experiences arises from narcissistic humiliations leading to embarrassment, shame, and anger.

The fear of the consequences differ for shame and guilt. The anxiety about shame is fear of abandonment by loved ones. Guilt, on the other hand, leads to fear of punishment.

Piers and Singer (1953) indicate a relationship between guilt and narcissism when they describe the ego ideal as having a core af narcissistic omnipotence with a magical belief that one is invulnerable. When we do something that threatens our magical fantasy of immortality, we condemn ourselves and feel guilty.

This is really a good definition of narcissistic guilt. The concern about the shame is associated with a fear of contempt, or at a higher social level, anxiety about exposure, and ostracism by the group.

Freud in "On Narcissism" (1914) also related the ego ideal to narcissism:

This ideal ego is not the target of the self-love which was enjoyed in childhood by the actual ego. The subject's narcis-

sism makes its appearance displaced onto this new ideal ego which, like the infantile ego, finds itself possessed of every perfection that is of value.

He goes on to point out that we are not willing to give up the narcissistic perfection of our childhood and we continue to strive for it in the ego ideal. It is really a replacement for the lost narcissism of our childhood in which we were our own ideal.

In his numerous discussions of feelings of guilt and shame, Freud generally speaks of shame with reference to sexual feelings and guilt to hostile impulses. In accordance with this concept, if we feel we have done something that reflects on our childhood ideal of narcissistic perfection, we feel both ashamed and that we have done something wrong. These are combined in what I am calling narcissistic guilt.

Helen Lewis (1971) points out that shame and guilt may both arise from a moral transgression and tend to be combined under the label of guilt. For the same act one may feel ashamed of oneself and also feel guilty. The shame reaction would include thoughts such as "How could *I* have done that; what an idiot I am—how humiliating; what a fool—how mortifying." The guilty thoughts would be "How could I have *done* that; what an injurious thing to do; how I hurt so-and-so; what will become of that or him now that I have neglected to *do it* or injured *him*. How should I be punished or make amends. *Mea Culpa!*"

There is a large gray area in which it is not clear whether we feel we have done something wrong or have not achieved an ideal goal, and usually it is both. A person in this situation ruminates and worries about what he or she did, feeling that he or she did a very stupid or foolish thing, blaming himself or herself, and feeling very guilty about it. There is anger involved as well, the anger being turned against oneself for having done this to oneself.

PAUL

When Paul came to see me, he was depressed and kept repeating, "I have only myself to blame, no one else."

Paul was referred by his internist who was treating him for advanced emphysema (a disease of the lungs in which the lung tissue has lost its elasticity and the person has great difficulty breathing). Through his labored breathing, he told the following story: He had been a storekeeper under continual tension. He was a chain cigarette smoker, and about fifteen years earlier his doctor had cautioned him that if he did not stop smoking, he would develop a serious lung disease. He continued to smoke and gradually developed the emphysema that led to his first hospitalization about two years ago. When he finally realized how sick he was, he stopped smoking. The emphysema progressed, however, so that by the time I first saw him, he was unable to do any kind of physical activity and required oxygen during the day because of his diseased lungs. He kept berating himself, saying how stupid he had been not to have listened to his doctor.

He lamented, "I feel so guilty, but I am totally responsible. I can't blame anyone but myself."

Paul had a combination of a physical disease (emphysema), which was affecting the oxygen supply to his body and brain, plus an emotional problem. He was suffering from narcissistic guilt, feeling he had brought this disaster on himself. Moreover, he was depressed because he was furious with himself for not having listened to his doctor. Paul had to recognize fully and deal not only with his guilt feelings but also his angry feelings, which he was directing toward himself.

Family Narcissistic Guilt

We have been discussing narcissistic guilt at the level of the individual. It also extends to the family group and is related to the "what will people think?" school.

Mother says, "You came home late last night and sat on the porch smoking pot with your boyfriend. What will the neighbors think?" You are made to feel guilty, not only for having disgraced yourself but also for embarrassing the family.

The young man who is arrested for possession of drugs has not only done wrong and harmed himself but, in addition, he is told he has also brought disgrace upon the family, thereby adding to his feelings of guilt.

Perhaps the best example of the power of this form of family guilt is seen among Japanese people. There is an unusually high incidence of adolescent suicide in Japan. Studies have shown that many of these young people have sought admission to the prestigious Japanese universities and if they fail to be accepted, they feel they have not only humiliated themselves but also have "lost face" for the family. They develop such guilt that they commit suicide. They believe this will relieve the guilt, not only through self-punishment, but also because this act has taken on the honorable overtones of "saving face" as seen in the historical role of hara-kiri. It seems like a drastic solution but indicates the strength of the guilt feelings.

Social Narcissistic Guilt

At a yet broader level, there is the guilt felt by a member identifying himself or herself with a social group. This may range from a neighborhood, to cities, and to nations. There are still residents of Dallas who feel guilty because President John F. Kennedy was killed in their city. This identification with the group carries with it the implication that the individual could somehow have prevented it or perhaps at a deeper level of consciousness had participated in some fashion in the event. In New York, many people felt guilty when the newspapers reported the story of a young woman who was attacked and murdered while a number of individuals stood around and did nothing to help her.

On the national level, there are people who feel guilty because we invaded Grenada. They may be angry, too, because they feel we did wrong and in identifying with the United States, take upon themselves the guilt for the invasion.

We identify with other groups as well. The Irish may feel guilt whenever an Irishman commits a crime. There were Jews who were greatly relieved that the man who attempted to assassinate President Reagan was not Jewish. Many blacks become upset (see Madow 1972) whenever a black man is charged with a violent crime. They resent it, are frightened by it, and feel guilty that it was "one of their own." These are guilt feelings related to something having been done to bring shame or humiliation on oneself or one's group.

Another aspect of narcissistic guilt is specifically related to anger. A person feels that he may have acted in a way that may have antagonized someone; that person will, in turn, be angry with him, and this will be painful and frightening for the individual. This person worries about the fear that he may have unintentionally hurt someone. The innocent action may have led to a person or object being harmed; the person will be worried he will be seen as hostile. The narcissistic guilt is a feeling that one did something which is going to lead to harm, belittlement, or embarrassment. He obsesses about his act and feels guilty. It is a variation of the obsessional fear that one's hostile impulses will be revealed. In narcissistic guilt the fear is one of mortification, embarrassment, a narcissistic injury, in contrast to the fear of punishment and retaliation.

There is a painful area involving sexual feelings that one may worry will lead to embarrassment. We have guilt about the possibility that we may have revealed an interest in sex. This leads to anxiety about how others will react toward us because of these sexual needs.

Blushing reflects this concern. We blush because we are upset that some thoughts or feelings that we are ashamed of have become known. Rather than providing relief, the red face accentuates the embarrassment because people will comment about it and seem to be laughing at us. When they indicate that we seem sensitive about something that is now revealed, we experience further feelings of chagrin and embarrassment.

The *fear* of blushing is another matter. There is a rare

neurotic entity called erythrophobia, which is not a condition of excessive blushing but rather a fear of blushing. It is a special problem related to blushing, and most people who blush do not suffer from it. Analysts have found that the psychodynamics involved include a fear of displaying an engorged red organ (the erect penis), which is then displaced upward. Behind the fear is the wish. The fear is that by displaying the red face, we are really exposing our organ, which is our wish. It is a form of exhibitionism, clearly forbidden to the erythrophobic's conscience. Every time the person with this condition blushes, he feels guilty because it is revealing his unacceptable desire to exhibit himself. This results in the fear that the wish will break through.

MARTIN

Martin came to see me because he was suffering from erythrophobia. He was 30 years old, a handsome, single, insurance broker, who worked in a large office where there were many secretaries. He did not date, however, because he was so afraid he would blush. In fact, he always went to work early and stayed late in his office because he was afraid that if he walked out among the secretaries, he would blush.

He confessed, "When I blush, I feel like a red light in front of a whorehouse."

One day during a treatment session he made the following slip of the tongue, "Whenever I have to walk past all those secretaries, I always check to make sure my fly is *open* — I mean closed."

As treatment progressed, he became aware of his guilt feelings about wanting to be admired and his wish to exhibit himself. Once he understood that behind his fear was his wish, he was able to accept his sexual feelings and find more realistic outlets for them.

Parental guilt, feelings that have reached significant proportions in recent years, consists of several types of guilt. One is narcissistic guilt. The parents are humiliated and demeaned by their children's behavior. They feel guilty and assume responsibility for it. The child's behavior reflects on them.

JANE

A 40-year-old housewife told this story: "Whenever I take my four sons to visit my mother-in-law, she prepares cocoa for them. They take this as a matter of fact and show little appreciation. My mother-in-law complains, 'How is it that the boys don't make a fuss about my cocoa? I fix it especially for them, and they don't appreciate it.' I tell her that I fix cocoa every night and that it's no special treat. My mother-in-law is hurt and tells me they are being reared without discipline. Then I feel guilty about it all.

"My mother-in-law is implying that I'm not training the boys properly to appreciate good things that are done for them. I find I am doubting myself and wondering whether or not I am a good mother, feeling the guilt laid on me by my mother-in-law. She makes me feel inadequate as a mother. I have never been that secure about it anyway, and my guilt is tremendous!"

This woman had accepted her mother-in-law's judgment and was struggling not only with her narcissistic guilt but also with her anger against her mother-in-law, which she feels she has no right to have. She then turns the anger against herself, increasing the guilt feelings as further self-punishment.

In addition to narcissistic guilt, there is guilt over the anger stirred up in parents because a child is a problem; for example when parents discover their son or daughter is homosexual. They resent the child, feel guilty for feeling this way, and deny it, even to themselves. This guilt has been well outlined in parents of handicapped children (Group for the Advancement of Psychiatry 1963). When parents are confronted with what might seem to be the obvious fact that they have a retarded or handicapped child, their initial reaction can be one of denial. Denial is one of the unconscious psychological mechanisms of defense. The problem is treated as if it does not exist:

"This cannot be."

"The doctors are wrong."

At this point, many families begin "medical shopping." They look for a physician who will tell them either that the other doctors are wrong and the child is normal or that even if the child is somewhat retarded, he or she will "grow out of it."

When additional consultants arrive at the same conclusion, other reactions appear. Guilt feelings arise as they consider what they might have done to produce this handicap. Since these ideas are painful, it is not unusual for another mechanism of defense to be utilized—projection of the blame onto others. Frequent targets for this blame are the spouse, in-laws, obstetrician, or pediatrician. The parents may not be aware of their guilt feelings because they are dealing with them through projection.

The frequent appearance of some transient conscious or unconscious guilt feelings in the parents of handicapped children is understandable; they reason that if the infant is defective, the fault must be theirs. Anger in having to carry this burden may also occur but is frequently denied, and further guilt is developed.

Not infrequently, the parents wish to be rid of the problem child. Now they feel guilt for having such feelings, and the guilt is further repressed.

In an effort to deny the anger and guilt, parents often rely on a mechanism of defense called "reaction formation" in which they bend over backwards to care for the child and are overly concerned about any injury and illness. This is a part of their denial of the wish to rid themselves of the handicapped child.

Parents of an emotionally disturbed child often feel they caused the child's emotional problems and that others have judged them and found them guilty. This type of guilt may be seen in a variety of circumstances. Two examples were Charles and Mrs. Cook.

CHARLES

Charles, a 46-year-old lawyer, had decided to start his own practice. He struggled against the competition of the large established law firms and found his income was limited.

Because of other expenses, he had not had sufficient funds to send his only daughter to a private school, something he felt was essential so that eventually she would acquire the "right" husband. She became withdrawn, and Charles attributed this to her not having the opportunities to socialize with what he considered to be desirable friends. He felt guilty, blaming himself for her difficulties, but his need to establish himself as an independent practitioner drove him to continue, despite his financial difficulties. He felt completely responsible for his daughter's emotional problems. He had been reared in an upper-class, high-achieving family and was humiliated and hurt by his daughter's inadequacies.

When she was 17 years old, the daughter ran off with a drug-addicted musician in her class at school. Charles panicked. He went driving in the streets at random, hoping to find her. He was terrified that his parents would find out, disapprove, and place the blame on him. His father had wanted him to go into their best friend's law firm where he would have been assured financial success. Then he could have afforded to send his daughter to a "good" school, and this situation would not have occurred.

When Charles finally heard from his daughter, she was in Chicago, and he took the next plane out to get her. She was actively hallucinating and was eventually diagnosed as having schizophrenia (the cause of which is not known for certain). Charles continued to feel that it was all his fault, and overwhelmed by his guilt feelings, he became depressed. It was not until he was able to deal with his narcissistic guilt and his rebellion against his family as well as his rage that this could happen to him, that he could see what was actually going on with his daughter and deal with it realistically.

MRS. COOK

Mrs. Cook was a 55-year-old woman whose 23-year-old son had been having a number of emotional problems including violent temper outbursts and an inability to concentrate on his school work. These resulted in his being dropped by several schools and his being unable to hold a job. He moved out of the house, demanded money from his mother for support, and repeatedly blamed her for his situation. Mrs. Cook was consumed with guilt because she felt her son was justified in placing the blame on her and that all his problems did, indeed, stem from her actions. She had worked hard as a young woman to put her husband through architectural school. After he became successful, he had an affair with a younger woman. When Mrs. Cook found out about it, she divorced him, furious that he could do this to her after all her sacrifices for him.

When her son began having emotional difficulties, she internalized her anger, feeling she was hasty in seeking the divorce and blaming herself. "It must have been my fault," she said.

She spent most of her money seeking help for her son, feeling she deserved nothing for herself because she was responsible for his difficulties. Recently, she had visited her son's psychiatrist, and it seemed to her that he practically said her son's difficulties were due to her mishandling of him. She became so depressed that she was unable to function and was persuaded by her sister to seek help.

With treatment, Mrs. Cook was able to see that she was furious with her husband for his lack of appreciation for what she had done for him and for abandoning her. She was hurt and angry at her son for making her feel guilty. She was also able to express her rage at her son's psychiatrist who, she felt, had added to her guilt.

Narcissistic guilt may be a major factor keeping people from seeking the psychiatric help they need. They are afraid that what they must tell the doctor will reflect badly on them, and rather than expose themselves, they stay away. Once in treatment, the patient may have difficulty expressing his or her thoughts for fear of humiliation. The patient needs to accept the fact that the psychiatrist is not passing judgment. The task of therapy is to discover and resolve the problems together.

6

Healthy Guilt

In discussing the problem of guilt, we have focused on the overreaction of guilt to a variety of situations. This is the common problem in most people with well-developed consciences. However, the opposite can also occur. There are individuals who apparently do not have sufficient guilt in situations which do call for such a reaction. They are lacking in what can be called healthy guilt.

There is a group of people who are diagnosed as sociopaths or psychopaths (official diagnosis: Antisocial Personality Disorder). These individuals are believed to have an insufficient, inadequate, or a complete lack of conscience. They commit serious crimes against society with no feelings of guilt. At first, it was thought that these people had an inborn disposition or a constitutional factor that caused them to behave in this fashion. In fact, at one time they were called constitutional psychopathic inferior (CPI). There are still some who believe in this theory and are looking for genetic factors such as the XYY chromosome defect to explain criminal behavior.

Adelaide Johnson (1952) described "superego lacunae," meaning "holes in the conscience." Individuals with superego lacunae can perform all sorts of antisocial acts without guilt. They are unable to form meaningful relationships or loyalties to groups. They are frequently callous toward others' feelings. Their behavior usually cannot be modified by punishment. There is a failure to develop a socially adapted superego and ego ideal.

In the American Psychiatric Association's manual, DSM-III (1980), the Antisocial Personality Disorder is described as follows:

There is a history of continuous and chronic behavior in which the rights of others are violated. Lying, stealing, fighting, truancy, and resisting authority are typical early childhood signs. In adolescence, unusually early or aggressive sexual behavior, excessive drinking, and use of illicit drugs are frequent. In adulthood, this kind of behavior continues with additional inability to sustain consistent work performance, or to function as a responsible parent, and failure to accept social norms with respect to lawful behavior. Almost invariably there is markedly impaired capacity to sustain lasting, close, warm, and responsible relationships with family, friends, or sexual partners.

The antisocial personality reflects an extreme lack of, or a very defective conscience. People with such a disorder may be seen in all walks of life from petty criminals to highly successful businessmen who defraud their companies. Strictness of conscience varies. Some individuals are fairly free in how they interpret right from wrong, while others are overly scrupulous about doing the right thing. How many people would steal or commit other crimes if they felt certain that they would not be caught?

Most of us find ourselves at times in the position of trying to decide whether to do something that we know is wrong, knowing that the odds are that no one will ever know.

Jean Jacques Rousseau, the great French philosopher and writer of the eighteenth century, gave a beautiful example when he asked the reader what he would do if — without leaving Paris and, of course, without being discovered — he could kill, with great profit to himself, an old mandarin in Peking by a mere thought. Rousseau suggests that he would not give much for the life of that dignitary. *Tuer son mandarin* (to kill his mandarin) became a popular phrase for this secret readiness in most people.

The whole issue of how comfortable people are about cheating is reviewed in an amusing but sobering article, "Everybody Does It" by Philip Longman (1984). He lists the various types of cheaters and speaks of the cheating epidemic that is sweeping America. He says that the varieties of cheating are almost inexhaustible.

Examples are the "defensive cheats" who claim that they must cheat on their income tax because everyone else does and the "self-righteous cheats" who cheat because they believe they are right. Longman cites the incident in Houston where the city's school teachers were required to take competency tests. They openly cheated because they felt the test was an insult to their profession. Almost 10 percent of the nation's undergraduates believe that some forms of cheating are necessary to get the grades they want.

The article goes on to say that the modern cheater will always have a certain cold logic. "With his own deceit, he brings to himself immediate, certain, and usually easy gains, seemingly at the expense of no one, or at least no one in particular, thus feeling no guilt about it."

Longman suggests that we have become a nation of cheats. This is undoubtedly related to the standards of behavior that are set by our leaders, as well as other authority figures in our society, from our presidents on down. In a nation accustomed to reading about presidential appointees rejected for illegal acts, openly lying, destroying important documents, or not disclosing conflicts of interest, it is difficult to point a finger at those who pad their expense reports or take home pencils from work. Do these national representatives lack sufficient healthy guilt?

On April 28, 1988, the Philadelphia *Inquirer* reported on its front page an incident that had occurred at a New York bank. The automated teller machine had been erroneously programmed and instead of $5 bills it dispensed $20 bills, so that if you requested $200 in cash you received $800.

One person reported that he had called everyone he knew to come down and a long line of eager cardholders quickly formed. There was a whole range of reactions. One person hollered with joy; another made a speech about getting back at the bank for money it owed *her*.

When one person called to report the problem, the branch manager reflected, "I was really surprised the gentleman called."

The article asked the reader to decide what he/she would do on receiving this gift. Would you alert the bank, would you "take the money and run," or would you call your friends to share in this bonanza? The reporter declared that if you informed the bank you would be a "rare breed of cat." There was apparently no guilt among the participants. What would you have done?

Leo Rangell writes about Richard Nixon and his behavior in *The Mind of Watergate, an Exploration of the Compromise of Integrity* (1980). He feels that what was appearing at the top level of government was a reflection of what was latent and widespread in the entire population; Nixon was a product of his times. He describes how Nixon would lie "without the friction of guilt . . . Nixon's fascinating capacity to discharge aggression without guilt" is what made him attractive to the people.

"Guilt," writes Rangell, "is a widespread internal oppressor. People are intrigued by one who shows them that their self-torments are not necessary." He goes on to point out that most of us have a superego that controls our ego but Nixon's ego had free reign, allowing him to do as he pleased. Rangell makes two basic points:

- Nixon had no conscience.
- Many people in this country secretly admired Nixon for that lack.

It is important that we all feel guilt about things that are maladaptive. The key word is maladaptive. Should we feel guilty about "little white lies"? I believe it depends on how harmful they are. Many stories have been written about the reality that one cannot go for 24 hours without telling a white lie. The implication is that the white lie is a socially useful mechanism.

Healthy guilt is the guilt that controls our behavior so that our society can function most effectively, i.e., if you feel guilty because you want to harm or cheat someone, or to violate a law the violation of which interferes with effective social functioning and the survival of the society, that is healthy guilt.

A pharmacist who has given a patient a wrong prescription

that made that person ill should, indeed, feel guilty. If he does not, he does not have sufficient healthy guilt. If he becomes severely depressed and tries to commit suicide, his reaction has become excessive.

In addition to those having an antisocial personality, there are several groups of people who lack healthy guilt. The first group consists of the narcissistic individuals who are so self-centered that they feel entitled to take anything they want and expect others to do whatever they desire without consideration of the others' needs or feelings. The narcissist often has no sense of guilt about making such demands or about transgressing other peoples' rights or properties.

ALICE

Alice was a 22-year-old, attractive young woman who had dropped out of college, was unable to hold a job, and continued to press her father for extra money. When he decided to stop supporting her, she became depressed and cut her wrists in a suicide gesture.

Alice's parents were divorced when she was 3 years old, and she was reared by her mother. Her mother doted on her, and Alice could do no wrong. At an early age Alice stole money from her mother's purse for candy and other trivial things. Her mother ignored this for years but eventually disciplined her. Alice became furious and complained that her allowance was not big enough. Alice's father, who felt guilty about abandoning Alice, indulged her with expensive presents and money.

Alice felt rules did not apply to her. If she did not feel like going to school, she stayed home with some feeble excuse that her mother readily accepted. By the time she was old enough to date, she was quite attractive, but she expected the boys to cater to her every whim and as a result, they usually dropped her. In college she felt no need to work at her studies and soon quit. Her father, a successful businessman with many business friends, obtained a job for her, but she would come late or be absent at will. She refused to do work that she said was beneath her. This attitude undermined the morale of the other employees. She was fired and lost several other jobs for similar reasons. Her father purchased a small townhouse for her. She demanded expensive furnishings, which, at first, he supplied. When she insisted on a costly hi-fi system, he refused and informed her that he would no longer support her. That is when she made the suicide gesture. She had never felt guilt about her excessive demands, believing these things were due her.

A second large group of people who appear to have relatively little guilt comprises those who are extremely angry and, at times, may not even be consciously aware of their rage. These people have so much anger against others that they feel no guilt if they harm someone. They get gratification from expressing the rage, since it releases the anger and gives them the satisfaction of seeing someone else hurt. These are often people who have been severely emotionally deprived as children and physically abused. They have no guilt about stealing, or attacking someone or, because they are so angry, abusing their own children.

A third class, related to the second, is the group reared by standards different from those the general society is accustomed to. These are people who have been financially deprived or raised in underprivileged circumstances and have been taught basically that the important thing is survival. A teenager who had been arrested for robbing and viciously assaulting his victim said in a television interview, "My mother never taught me it was wrong to take from others. I was taught to survive!" Whatever needs to be done to survive seems justified to these people, and they feel no guilt about it. The only concern they have is the fear of being caught and punished. They are not acting in anger but behaving according to the standards they have been taught.

These individuals' reactions are not to be confused with the behavior initiated by psychosis. The psychotic individual is reacting to his or her own illness, which generates delusions, hallucinations, and paranoid ideas; such a person responds to those ideas, which may include the need to attack or murder other people. Psychotics have no guilt about their actions because in their delusional system, their behavior seems appropriate.

JOHN

A famous case in Norristown, Pennsylvania, became known as "The Case of the Evil Eye Killer."

I evaluated the mental status of a prisoner named John, charged with murdering six people because he said they were witches. John was a pasty-faced man of average build, who, as soon as I entered the room, began talking with a great flow of speech, somewhat disjointedly, but returning frequently to his main theme of witchcraft. When asked questions, he would answer politely and accurately, but would return very quickly to the topic of witches, hexing, and the evil eye.

John was of Italian descent, the oldest of four children. He was 28 years old then. He had completed the ninth grade when he was taken out of school to care for his mother and year-old sister. John had assisted at the birth of this child. The mother had had a nervous breakdown afterwards. He believed that the witches' evil trickery had begun when one of them had placed some red-colored magical object in their toilet where his mother had delivered the baby.

The mother was hospitalized in Norristown State Hospital; and John's life consisted of going to school, coming home, and sitting in his room alone. He said that the happiest time of his life was when he left home to enter the army. In reality he was able to function in the army for only two weeks and then was hospitalized in a neuropsychiatric ward. He described his stay in the hospital as very pleasant, and he was happy there. He received fifteen electrical shocks. After six months in the service, he was released with a medical discharge.

Most of my interview was focused on John's somewhat disconnected but fixed recital of the various episodes of his family's life connected with witches, hexes, and the evil eye *(mal occhio)*. John assured me that his father was an expert in this field and had taught him all about it. His father and mother believed in witchcraft. He indicated that witches do not use ordinary weapons; they use secret words and needles in dolls. He said, "If you kill the witch, it sets you free." When he was asked if he would kill anyone else, he said, "No, just the people my father told me about."

One of the couples that John had killed was childless. They had offered to care for the new sister while his mother was hospitalized. John's family concluded that they must have conspired with the other witches to drive his mother crazy in order to get her baby. His father said that the witches put poison in the family's food and that they had a grudge against him because they were jealous that he would become a wealthy man.

John declared, "If I knew who was putting the hex on me, and it kept up, I would continue killing until it stopped."

He complained about difficulty in breathing and a feeling he was being suffocated. He said, "They are doing this to me!"

"It was like living in purgatory," he insisted, "and I studied how to do it to get rid of their torturing me and my mother. If I could get their hex curse off of me, I'd be normal."

John complained, "I have always lived in fear. I have been afraid to make friends. My mother cursed and hollered and scared the whole family. I was afraid to talk to people. When I came home, I heard nothing but nonsense talk. I got so scared, I lost weight. There was another witch, Anthony, who caused my sister Rose to have a paralyzed leg. They are like the Mafia, but they are supernatural. They do not use guns. The only way to handle them is to kill them."

John showed the signs and symptoms of a paranoid schizophrenic disorder. He was accused of killing six elderly people over a period of six years, declared insane, and sent to a hospital for the criminally insane.

Did John feel guilty about killing these six elderly people? It was clear that he did not. Actually, he felt that he was ridding society of evil persons. At one point he told me that, rather than being put in prison, he should be rewarded for having done these good deeds.

If a psychotic person such as John truly believes that he is performing an act as a result of a command from God or a fixed idea that these people are dangerous, evil, or plotting against him, then he will feel no guilt about disposing of them in any way he can. John had many guilt feelings about taking care of his mother and about obeying his father but not about killing these six people because they were witches. He had to get rid of them.

An interesting sidelight occurred when the neighborhood where John lived was canvassed. Many of the people living there believed in witches. When asked how one gets rid of a witch, most replied that the only way was to kill the witch. When they were asked whether they, themselves, would kill a witch, they replied, "No, it is against the law." When these neighbors were questioned about what they thought of John, they replied, "He's crazy!"

These people had developed superegos unimpaired by psychosis and were able to recognize that killing is a crime. In spite of their belief in the evil eye, they had sufficient healthy guilt to control their wish to kill (Foulks and colleagues 1977).

Healthy guilt comes from a well-developed conscience. It is the type of guilt that influences our behavior so that we function as social beings, considerate of others. An adequate healthy guilt level acts as a deterrent to maladaptive behavior. It keeps us from acting on impulses that can be harmful and fosters a safe society.

The resolution of intrapsychic conflict does not mean we must not have wishes that may be antisocial. We must accept that such wishes exist in all of us, but we need sufficient superego strength in order not to act on them.

There are some who feel that unless more people develop a greater sense of healthy guilt, our social structures may be threatened. Dr. Judd Marmor, in a speech before the American Association of Social Psychiatry in Chicago, May 12, 1987, emphasized the social and cultural factors in postulating his reasons for a decline in decency and moral values, what we are describing as an inadequate amount of healthy guilt. He blamed lack of family organization, faulty parental attitudes, the influence of television, and the noncaring for the underprivileged, in addition to the intrapsychic conflicts that occur in the individual's personality development. He indicated that our society is reverting to "the values of the jungle."

Too much or too little guilt can be harmful for the individual and society. Unhealthy types of guilt can be difficult to deal with, and may require professional help. It is usually easier to treat the individual with an excessive guilt-reaction than the one lacking guilt, because the overreaction is usually related to forbidden impulses we all have but may not be able to accept. Once these impulses become known and are accepted as normal human drives, they can be dealt with appropriately. This decreases the pathological guilt. People who have relatively little guilt are not motivated to change because they feel no pain or guilt about their actions. Their major concern is being caught and punished.

Benjamin Karpman (1956) is more optimistic. He believes that criminality is a symptom of psychosis. The antisocial behavior results from a disturbed instinctive and emotional life produced by early environmental influences. If this is so, it should be possible to treat people with this disorder psychotherapeutically.

Unfortunately, as several studies have shown, stricter laws do not generally deter the criminal who has no sense of guilt. Such a person believes his or her main task is to avoid apprehension. The normal population with a healthy sense of guilt is deterred by the stricter laws because of its more fully developed conscience. The person with an antisocial personality is merely more determined than ever not to be caught.

Some of these people may respond to treatment, but the long-term answer lies in prevention. It is essential that efforts be made in childrearing to develop sufficiently strong superegos that produce effective healthy guilt with regard to antisocial behavior. Appropriate standards of behavior need to be established early and proper role models are essential so that children and future adults will seek satisfaction in socially useful and acceptable ways. "If you need money, you don't steal it; you *earn* it!"

7

Unhealthy Guilt

Healthy guilt leads us to socialize our behavior and accept responsibility for our actions. Unhealthy guilt is maladaptive and interferes with the ability to function efficiently. We have discussed the lack of sufficient healthy guilt in the psychopathic person, which can threaten others and society. The other extreme is an excessive guilt reaction, which can cause personal suffering and interfere with normal daily living. This is the more common type of guilt and is the concern of most of this book.

When people feel guilty about something, they may be aware of it and suffer from pangs of conscience. They are miserable, request forgiveness, and may seek punishment or castigate themselves to relieve the painful feelings. As uncomfortable as these guilt feelings are, if one is aware of the guilt and what it is related to, it is possible to consider ways of dealing with it. The youngster who flunks a subject in school may feel guilty about it but has several options: be punished at home and promise to do better, resolve to improve, or be given extra work by the teacher to make up for the failure. On the negative side, the youngster may put all the blame on the teacher, or be truant to avoid facing the problem.

Often, however, one feels guilty about something, represses it, and is thereby no longer aware of the guilt feelings. Clinical signs and symptoms may result.

In the classic story "Rain," by Somerset Maugham, mentioned earlier, the Reverend Davidson felt so guilty about his sexual desires that he repressed both the sexual wishes and the guilt. The repressed feelings drove him to insist that everyone must control his or her sexual impulses. If you had asked how he felt about sex, he would probably have said it was an invention of the devil and vehemently denied any interest in it himself or any guilt feelings about it. When his own desire broke through, he was so overwhelmed that he committed suicide.

Guilt may manifest itself in the extreme form of having thoughts about suicide or in actually committing the act itself. One individual may believe that he or she committed an unpardonable act and, because of guilt, thinks about suicide. Another may have suicidal thoughts, unaware that he or she has denied any guilt feelings, and is only conscious of feeling suicidal.

CAL

Cal was a 6-foot-tall athletic 32-year-old computer expert who was referred for treatment because he had become depressed and was not functioning well at work. He said he had lost interest in his profession and no longer enjoyed anything in life including his marriage, his hobby of stamp collecting, and even his 3-year-old daughter. He said he was unable to account for his depression and wondered if it was a midlife crisis. He had suicidal thoughts, and they frightened him because he could not understand why he should be having such feelings.

Cal indicated that he was happily married to his college sweetheart, a young woman who had been much sought after by the men in his college class. He felt he was fortunate she chose him to be her husband. Cal described her as very attractive and sexually exciting. As the details were explored, it became clear that he was not really *that* happy in the marriage. From the start, his wife indicated to him that he was too interested in sex, and this made him feel like a "sexual maniac." He accepted her judgment and attempted to repress his sexual desire, stating frequently how lucky he was to have won the campus queen (a fact she reminded him of often) and what a wonderful woman she was. However, he revealed that she also complained about his desire to exercise and keep his body physically trim, belittling his interest in his own body. He expressed with intense feeling how he enjoyed singing in the shower until his wife would yell to him to stop, and he would. Somewhat apologetically he confessed that she was dissatisfied with his progress at work, feeling that by now he should have established his own computer company and become a millionaire. He accepted these criticisms, feeling that she was correct in her assessments of him. He strove to please her.

It was not until Cal had been in treatment for awhile that he was able to realize how furious he was with her for belittling him and making him feel like a freak. He had not been able to accept his rage at her, and feeling guilty about his anger, he had denied both the anger and the guilt to himself. Believing he had no right to be dissatisfied with anything she did, the guilt about the hostile feelings toward her for being critical and unloving caused him to repress them. This led to his depression and suicidal thoughts.

He expressed incredulity when I raised the question of whether or not it was possible that his sexual desires were normal and that perhaps his wife had a problem with sex. When we were able to bring out his guilt feelings about his own desires as well as his anger toward his wife, he began to feel relief. Further treatment was necessary for him to understand and deal with his belief that he had no right to be angry with his wife or to expect a sexually responsive partner.

Behind most neurotic reactions is pathological guilt. This may occur in people who do not even know they feel guilty. They have feelings that are unacceptable and feel guilty for having them. Both the original feeling and the guilt are repressed and appear as clinical symptoms.

HELEN

Helen was a 65-year-old married mother of two grown sons, who felt anxious, depressed, and inadequate because she was not satisfying all of the demands of her ailing 90-year-old mother. Her mother lived in a nearby apartment with a live-in companion. Helen felt it was important that she see her mother at least twice a day, prepare her meals, and call the doctor whenever her mother complained. She had been dominated by her mother all her life and was not aware of how much she hated her mother for her overprotection and excessive domination. Such resentment was not acceptable to Helen; she responded by being overly solicitous, attempting to take care of her mother's every need in an effort to deny her real wish to see her dead.

It was not until the mother became seriously ill that Helen was able to understand, through treatment, that she resented her mother and that her impending death came frighteningly close to the possibility of satisfying her basic wish to be rid of her. Her reaction of excessive concern about her mother's illness was her unconscious effort to deny the wish for her mother's death because she felt so guilty about it. Both the wish and the guilt were repressed. Helen was only aware of her excessive need to care for her mother. She said, "I realize I am overly solicitous, but I worry so much and become anxious if I do not check in on her frequently."

Phobias are excessive, persistent, and unreasonable fears that can sometimes control one's life. There are numerous phobias, from agoraphobia (an abnormal fear of being in open or public places) to xenophobia (fear of strangers or foreigners). Phobias are complex and may be due to a combination of emotional problems, conditioning, and contagion. If someone has a phobia about cats (ailurophobia), and if a cat leaps into his automobile while he is sitting in it and frightens him, he may develop a phobia about autos. Phobias have been treated with some success through behavior modification therapy. The problem with this type of treatment is that it does not get at the cause of the phobia but, rather, is a symptomatic cure.

Although there are many causes of phobias, often behind the abnormal fear is a forbidden wish. The wish must be hidden because we feel so guilty about it that we repress it. We then develop an abnormal fear of anything that might come close to satisfying that wish. Thus, we may be unaware of having guilt feelings but experience them as panic reactions, anxiety reactions, or phobic reactions.

The spinster who anxiously looks under her bed every night, frightened that a man might be hiding there, may not be doing it solely out of fear.

A person with a dirt phobia (mysophobia) may actually be fighting against his basic wishes to play with his feces and smear himself, but since this is forbidden, usually by parental decree, the person develops guilt feelings, denies the wish, and the wish is transformed into a dirt phobia. The individual is now focused on the fear and has no awareness of the wish or the guilt feelings about it.

A crowd phobia (ochlophobia) may be a means of coping with an unacceptable wish to do something in the crowd such as drawing attention to oneself by screaming an obscenity, or exposing oneself. Guilt makes the person push the wish into his or her unconscious, only to have it surface as a full-blown phobia.

Youngsters will say, "Step on a crack and break your mother's back!" This is another example of a fear and a guilt feeling about something related to a wish. Children carefully avoid stepping on a crack because they would feel guilty if something should happen to their mother as a result.

Religious leaders have been aware of the connection between phobias and guilt. Fulton Sheen (1949) writes: "There is nothing that so arouses unhealthy fear as hidden guilt."

Persons driven by obsessions and compulsions may be struggling with a similar problem. Individuals suffering from a particular compulsion will report, for example, that they have to straighten all pictures that are not aligned exactly. If they do not, they become anxious and panicky. They may even be able to admit that this does not make any sense and that they realize it is foolish. When one probes more deeply, it usually turns out that there is a hidden, hostile wish such as a desire that some harm befall someone they love. If they do not straighten out the picture, something will happen to that person. It is a defense against a wish that they feel guilty about and must deny. Once the wish is repressed, they need to develop a mechanism for keeping it in the unconscious. This is accomplished by creating a counteractive symptom, namely, one that the compulsive person feels will prevent the wish from being gratified. As long as the picture is straight, the unacceptable wish will not be fulfilled — for the moment — until the next crooked picture comes along.

Consider the following situation: You are furious at someone and shout, "Why don't you drop dead!" If that person did die suddenly, you would feel guilty because your wish was satisfied and *you* caused it to happen. This is the sort of unacceptable wish behind compulsive behavior as well as the phobias where a person tries by inadequate means to cope with a forbidden wish.

Many somatic disturbances may be seen as a result of guilt over unacceptable angry feelings that have been repressed. If anger is considered a form of energy, we know that it cannot be destroyed; and if it is repressed, it must come out somewhere. That we are unconsciously aware of this can be seen by our use of "organ language." Numerous expressions used to describe anger refer to the body without our being aware that they may be literally true (Madow 1972).

One person refers to someone as "a pain in the neck" because he is angry with him. Another goes to the doctor, complaining of a pain in the neck and may be expressing the same emotion, but is unaware of it. There are many causes for pain. When no organic cause is found, one should consider an emotional source.

A patient reported that on her way to my office she suddenly developed a severe pain in her rectum. She then thought about me, and the idea flashed through her mind, "He's a pain in the ass."

A mother says of her child who has misbehaved, "I am just itching to get my hands on him." Another mother may literally itch. One individual may say, "I just couldn't stomach him." Another becomes sick to her stomach without knowing why. These are all manifestations of anger about which we feel guilty and that we have denied but which then is expressed in somatic symptoms.

Articles and books have been written on the role of anger in psychosomatic disturbances such as ulcers, hypertension, and cardiac disease. In 1959, M. Friedman and R. H. Rosenman reported a study in which they were able to classify people into Type A and Type B personalities.

The Type A individual is intensely ambitious, competitive, preoccupied, and driven to meet deadlines. The Type B behavior pattern is the converse. Friedman and Rosenman found that the Type A personality was much more likely to have heart attacks.

Since 1959, many studies have been undertaken to determine more specifically which factors in the Type A person were most harmful. Margaret Chesney has edited a book with R. H. Rosenman (1985) reporting her research to cull out those causal features of the Type A individual that are linked to heart disease. The results were surprising. The ambitious, competitive, time-conscious Type A person was not harmed by those factors as much as by his or her *anger*.

The Type A person is always alert to challenges, often not trusting others, and, therefore, feeling hostile toward them. If another driver gets ahead of a Type A individual, it is a personal insult. This angry way of interpreting events has been linked with cardiovascular hyperactivity. Studies at Duke University have suggested that anger leads to actual narrowing of the coronary arteries. Another of Chesney's studies has shown that subjects who rated high on the anger questionnaire—individuals who often became angry, kept it in, and denied the anger—had persistently high blood pressure. Why do they repress the anger? There are many reasons. It may not be wise or practical to express it, and it may seem unjustified. Guilt or guilty fear can certainly be one of the reasons for the denial.

The alcoholic or drug abuser may be using those agents in an effort to relieve guilt feelings about some behavior or emotions that he or she feels are unacceptable.

LARRY

Larry was the 45-year-old manager of a women's clothing store who came to see me when he finally acknowledged that he had a drinking problem. He was missing days at work and had lapses of memory following a day of drinking. His wife told him that she was afraid of him when he was drunk because he became abusive.

Larry was a slightly built, youthful-looking man, who was shy and withdrawn. He volunteered little information and it required many questions to keep the interview going.

He was married to an author whom he described in glowing terms. "She is a wonderful person. She has a mind of her own, but she is the perfect wife." His story revealed that his spouse was a highly successful mystery writer, who earned twice the money he did. At first, he described her as most generous, buying him expensive clothing and other gifts. She insisted on managing her own funds, because she had a friend who was a successful investment counselor. Larry had recently thought that she was needling him for not being more successful financially. He said, "She has been so wonderful to me that whenever I feel like telling her off, I become so guilty about it that I hold the feelings in."

Larry was the oldest son of an overindulgent mother, whom he idolized and who constantly pointed out that his wife was not taking adequate care of him, working many evenings, attending lectures away from their home city, and worrying more about her editors than her husband.

Larry began drinking more and more, continuing to repress the anger about which he felt so guilty. When he became intoxicated, all of his rage and anger toward his wife came out, even though he swore that he had no memory of his behavior once he sobered up.

There are many other forms of unhealthy guilt. Some people experience guilt if they have *any* pleasurable experience. They do not feel they deserve a vacation or rewards and if they get them, they feel guilty believing they are not deserving. It is a derivative of the Puritan ethic suggesting that we must only work, not enjoy ourselves. A man recently said that every time he goes on vacation, he feels guilty because he isn't home working. Some people cannot enjoy receiving a gift, frequently indicating that they don't merit it. They feel uncomfortable for being given something that will provide them some pleasure.

Another type of unhealthy guilt occurs in people who feel that everything bad that happens is their fault, and they feel guilty over any incident in which they are involved. There may be a kernel of truth in the occurrence and this accentuates the guilt. During the war, a friend was scheduled to fly a mission in the Air Force and he became ill. His place was taken by another flyer and the plane was downed. All personnel were killed. My friend was devastated. He felt guilty about his friend's death, the fault being his because he should have gone on the mission. This is a variation of survivor guilt. An appropriate reaction of remorse and some guilt is understandable, but when these feelings persist and the individual continues to torment himself with guilt and insists on taking responsibility for the other flyer's death, it becomes unhealthy guilt.

There are reports of people who felt guilty because they believed they should have warned President Kennedy that he would be assassinated, and having failed to do so, believed that they had let him down and were overwhelmed by guilt. Many people feel guilty over the death or injury of a loved one, convinced that there was something they should have done to prevent it. A woman came to see me because she was feeling extremely guilty about her daughter's marriage. She had known the young husband since he was a child and when the marriage got into difficulty, she became obsessed with the idea that she should have known that this man was poor husband material and would make her daughter miserable. She continued to upbraid herself, saying, "I should have realized he was a mean person. It's all my fault that my daughter is now married to this evil man. Why didn't I stop it before it was too late?" Parents often take the entire blame for any difficulties their children have, feeling that it is their fault and that they should have been able to forestall the problems.

Unhealthy guilt, then, can cause clinical symptoms ranging from psychic pain over the guilt feelings to a variety of symptoms including depression, phobias, somatic disorders, and compulsions.

How does a person become aware of these guilt feelings? The guilt results from feelings the person has that are unacceptable. The desire to hurt someone, the wish to be rid of a burden, a forbidden sexual desire, the wish to be admired or made the center of everyone's attention are some examples. One can resolve the guilt feelings by becoming aware of what those unacceptable wishes and desires are. The suggestions in Chapter 10 can be helpful.

8

Guilt Producers

Which people and situations are likely to stir up guilt in everyone? At the top of the list of guilt producers are the persons who have been closest to us and with whom we have had the most exposure, our parents. All father has to do is give 4-year-old Johnny a look and he is overwhelmed with guilt. Mother says, "You have been a bad girl!" and 5-year-old Susie is filled with shame. Our parents are the people who are most important in establishing our standards of behavior and contributing to the development of our conscience. The standards, in turn, have come from religious codes, social customs, and laws, with individual variations introduced by our parents themselves.

Joe, a college student, lamented, "My father says I must study all the time. I'm not supposed to have fun, just work. I feel guilty if I'm not studying. I even feel guilty when I go home and talk to my father. I feel I should be studying and not wasting time talking to him."

Other authority figures can also generate guilt. Relatives such as older siblings, grandparents, aunts, and uncles can be guilt producers.

KATHY

Kathy worshiped her Aunt Sally, who was a beautiful and successful businesswoman. When she came to visit, Kathy hovered near her and fulfilled her least request. When Kathy visited her aunt, it was a thrilling experience. Her home was luxurious and there were fascinating things to see and do. Once when she was 9 years old, while visiting Aunt

Sally, she complained that her mother (Aunt Sally's sister) favored her older brother and did not pay any attention to her. Aunt Sally became annoyed with Kathy's criticism of her mother and told Kathy that she didn't appreciate her mother. Kathy was overwhelmed with shame and guilt and fear, feeling she had done something wrong and deserved her aunt's disapproval.

Teachers can also be significant guilt producers. It may be guilty fear or fear of punishment, but a teacher who is admired can generate true guilt. Erickson (1968) speaks of the use of shame and humiliation in teaching children as potentially harmful to the child. The youngster who is forced to stand in front of the class for not knowing an answer, especially if this ritual is done repeatedly and accompanied by the giggling and snickering of classmates, may be emotionally traumatized. He or she may develop feelings of inferiority and be unable to cope with criticism, or he or she may rebel and see how far he or she can defy authority and get away with it.

A second-grade teacher, who felt that Conrad had misbehaved, punished him by requiring him to use the girls' bathroom. The class howled with laughter. Conrad felt guilty for what he had done, but furious at the teacher for the punishment she had inflicted on him. He became more rebellious than ever and flatly refused to return to that school.

The police are well-known authority figures who can stir up guilt. Just the sight of the policeman makes some people uncomfortable. If they are driving along and suddenly see in the rear-view mirror a police car behind them, they feel guilty, certain they have done something wrong even if they have not.

Parental Guilt

Being a parent may also be a great guilt producer. Any problems that arise with children from birth defects to delinquency are assumed by some parents to be all their fault. This has not been helped by many of the psychological writings that suggest that whatever goes wrong emotionally with a child is due to poor parenting.

This assignment of responsibility has been a particularly heavy burden on the mother. Although no one can deny that good mothering is important in a child's upbringing, it is not the only factor that determines a child's character and personality. Freud himself placed a great emphasis on constitutional factors.

Thomas and Chess (1977) have shown, in a large long-term study, that children are born with their own temperaments, and they have described the "easy child," the "slow to warm up child," and the "difficult child." Parents of children who are not temperamentally easy feel erroneously that they are totally responsible for their children's personalities and develop guilt because the child is not ideally happy. Life's circumstances contribute a great deal to a child's development. The birth of other children, illness, or accidents, emotional traumas, moving from close friends, all may influence a child's emotional development. Erickson (1968) emphasizes psychosocial factors in a child's development.

Many working mothers today are struggling with guilt feelings about being away from home all day and "neglecting" their children because they must work to earn money or to feel fulfilled. They wonder whether they should have had children if they could not afford to stay home and care for them, or they castigate themselves, wondering whether they are entitled to seek satisfaction from work at the price of "sacrificing" the children. The decision to work need not be at the children's expense. It may be more difficult, but the children do not necessarily have to suffer.

For many years I taught at a women's medical school where there were a number of women physicians who were full-time teachers. They struggled with guilt feelings over what they feared was possible neglect of their children, which might result in warping their personalities. The medical students, too, had concerns about marrying and becoming mothers. They worried whether or not they could give their children a healthy upbringing if they spent time away from home practicing medicine.

The results I saw varied from excellent mothering to dismal failures; but the success or failure of the child's development did not usually depend upon the mothers alone. The cooperation of the father and his attitude toward his wife and family was equally important. The selection and availability of good housekeepers made a significant difference. All of the factors that influence a child's development played important roles, including schooling, peer pressures, and the youngster's own emotional needs. The individual woman's character, of course, played a significant part as well.

The working mother needs to make certain adjustments. The role of the mother in the first three years of the child's life is particularly important. If the mother can be available in those crucial years, helping the child to become an individual and to separate from his or her dependence on her, she will have given the child a good start. Father can be very helpful in this early phase of development as well. Arranging for a proper support system such as use of the extended family or a good day care center can continue the child's healthy progress.

Now with the increased number of divorces, there is a growing group of single parents who must work; some will feel even more guilty about their ability to provide what they perceive as adequate parenting for their children since they must be away from home all day, depriving the child of the only remaining parent.

Actress Glenda Jackson, in an interview discussing her son Danny, lamented, "I'm marked with maternal guilt for the rest of my life for not being home more when he was a baby and growing up. If anything goes wrong in Danny's life, I will always regard it as my fault."

Schools may contribute to parental guilt by reinforcing the idea that any difficulty a child is having in school is due to poor parenting. A young mother was called to school by her son Ronny's third-grade teacher, who complained that Ronny did not appear to be interested in reading and seemed detached from class.

The mother was horrified and overwhelmed with guilt. She knew Ronny was a bright child and enjoyed reading at home. The teacher said, "We have a whole table full of books that the children can select from and Ronny just passes them by." When the mother asked Ronny why he was not interested, he replied, "I looked them over, and I have read every one!" And he had! The teacher had not thought to inquire. School work can be boring to bright children. The boredom is not due to inadequate parenting.

As discussed previously, the parents of a handicapped child often feel guilty, believing that they had something to do with the child's unfortunate defect. Some parents react with guilt if inadequacies appear in their children, including failures at school, illnesses, injuries, or any other poor adjustment to life. This is not just confined to young children. The mother whose son or daughter fails to marry may feel it is all her fault and may develop a great deal of guilt over this. Parents of homosexuals often react with rage and guilt when they learn of their child's sexual choice (see Chapter 4).

Neglect

Feeling that one has neglected one's spouse and children can also be a guilt producer. The father who believes that he has been so preoccupied with his work that he has not paid sufficient attention to his family and is often reminded of this by his wife, may, in fact, develop guilt over these feelings.

The mother who goes to work may feel very guilty, fearing that she is neglecting her children and husband. When the children complain, "Mom is never home," and the husband expresses resentment that she is not available to make dinner, the woman may find herself feeling not only guilty but also angry, both at the unfairness of the accusation and the lack of cooperation and understanding on the part of the family. If the anger is unacceptable, it may generate further guilt. On the other hand, children may feel guilty over the way they have treated their parents.

PATTY

At the age of 18, Patty was constantly fighting with her mother. Father often found himself in the middle as the peace maker. The situation became so unbearable, Patty decided to move out and live with her boyfriend. Her parents were not pleased but reluctantly agreed. Father was quite unhappy and urged Patty to return home. Patty loved her father and was considering moving back when she received word that her father had been shot and killed at his place of business by burglars.

Along with the immediate shock at the loss, Patty was overwhelmed with guilt, feeling she should have been living at home and not have given her father so much grief. She even wondered if, somehow, she might have prevented his death. She berated herself, was unable to sleep, had a poor appetite, and began having suicidal thoughts. With the help of treatment, she was able to accept that she was overreacting and had in no way caused or contributed to his death.

Willard Gaylin, a psychiatrist at Columbia University, adds another dimension to death as a guilt producer. In an interview in the *New York Times* (February 5, 1985), he discussed the role of ambivalent feelings toward the death of a loved one.

> *Ambivalence is most likely to lead to pathological guilt when it is accompanied by a strong psychological dependence on the person who has died.*
> *If you feel you need the other person to cope with life, then they threaten your very survival by dying. You feel abandoned, but when you get angry at them, it triggers guilt over your anger.*

Gaylin goes on to say that the anger turned inward leads to depression, which serves as a form of punishment for the unacceptable angry feelings.

It is important to be aware of our own death wishes, particularly if we are furious with someone and wish he or she would die and then that person does die. Hostile wishes alone do not cause action, but if they are fulfilled, through no fault of ours, we may still feel guilty about them.

Suicide of a family member or a close friend may generate excessive guilt in the survivors. They may believe that there was something they could have done to prevent it. They should have recognized how unhappy that individual was and been more supportive; or, as in the case of Bill, they may feel that they were a contributing cause.

BILL

Bill, a 35-year-old product of the late 1960s hippy era, was depressed, felt life was meaningless, and felt that he had no future. He had grown up as an only child in a wealthy home, attended private schools, and was spoiled by his mother. His father was an ambitious, hard-working executive in the family business who insisted on strict discipline and a Spartan life for his son.

When Bill went out of town to college, he felt free of his father's domination and soon joined the drinking, marijuana-smoking group that also experimented with many of the hallucinogenic drugs. His grades were marginal and once he was placed on probation. In his junior year he received a phone call from his mother telling him that his father had committed suicide.

Bill was devastated. He had always thought of his father as a tower of strength who would live forever. Despite the fact that he later learned that his father had begun to drink heavily and was beset by business pressures, Bill began blaming himself for his father's death, believing that he had let his father down by his behavior in college. He became convinced that his father's disappointment in him had led to his suicide.

Bill dropped out of school and went home to live with his mother. He became so depressed that she took him to a psychiatrist, who prescribed antidepressant medication. He was then able to return to college and complete the work. His father had left a large trust fund for him but he was unable to touch the money, continuing to feel that he had been the cause of his father's suicide.

Bill wandered from job to job and now at age 35 recognized that he needed further psychiatric help. During a course of intensive psychotherapy, Bill became aware of the many feelings he had toward his father, including his love for him, his rage at his domination, the loss he felt, and the anger at him for deserting him through the suicide.

At the other end of the spectrum is the enormous guilt felt while contemplating euthanasia for someone. Aside from the medical and legal aspects, if a loved one is terminally ill, in pain, or comatose, we still feel guilt at the thought of taking away his or her life. Inflicting death, even if all indications are that it is appropriate, stirs up many conflicting emotions. Guilt feelings often result. If a loved one is suffering from incurable pain and begs to be allowed to die, the person whose conscience does not permit him or her to satisfy the wish, may also feel guilt for *prolonging* the suffering. It becomes a no-win situation.

Survivors of shared violent experiences may also develop feelings of guilt. Those who withstood the tortures of the Holocaust are an outstanding example. Following World War II, many survivors of the concentration camps had to receive professional help because of their guilt for having lived through the ordeals of the camp, having witnessed so many others perish. It became known as survivor guilt. It also occurs in soldiers returning from the war but whose buddies were killed. Survivor guilt may be seen in civilian life as well. I recently saw a young man who was involved in an automobile accident in which his two best friends were killed. He came to therapy because he was depressed and had tremendous guilt feelings because he had survived the accident and his friends had not.

One of the cruelest instances of guilt about death is the situation in which a mother dies at childbirth and the child is told frequently by the father that it is his or her fault that the mother died. The child grows up overwhelmed with the guilt of having caused the mother's death. In addition, there is frequently anger at the father for unfairly placing this responsibility on the child.

Failure

Failure may generate guilt. This can range from failing in school to a failure in business or achievement.

Healthy guilt can be useful if a student has failed an examination. It can be used to make the youngster work harder. If excessive guilt is generated, it may interfere with the student's functioning efficiently, and he or she may do even less well. Sometimes parents are unaware of this process, and by being overly harsh, hope to stimulate the child to study harder. Usually, this defeats their purpose and the child does even less work.

LESTER

Lester was a 28-year-old housepainter who was unhappy in his marriage and was having extramarital affairs but felt guilty about them.

His father was a high school teacher who was disappointed in his own achievements in life. He was determined that his son would do better. When Lester was still in elementary school, his father kept emphasizing how important grades were. When he brought home a poor report card, his father went into a rage. Lester was overwhelmed with fear and guilt. His father never praised his achievements but always criticized and threatened him when his work was not satisfactory.

Lester continued to fail in school. "I was terrified of my father," he said, "but couldn't help myself. I realized I was letting him down, and I felt so guilty." He began to cry. "I guess I feel sorry for myself, and I hate him for what he did to me."

Lester's father decided that he needed more discipline and sent him to a strict military school. Lester continued the same behavior. He did not do his homework and responded to the discipline by withdrawing more. After one year, the school recommended that he leave. He returned to a public school and as soon as he was of legal age, he dropped out. He said sorrowfully, "I hated school and couldn't wait to get out. As soon as I graduated, I got a job as a painter and have been doing it ever since. I married when I was 19, and you're not going to believe this, but my wife is just like my father. She tries to run my life, criticizes me incessantly. She makes me feel so guilty all the time, and I guess I'm rebelling against her just as I did against my father."

A special form of failure is a failure to remember. Many people are tormented by guilt for forgetting someone's birthday, a wedding anniversary, or an appointment. It is easy enough to understand why one might forget a dentist's appointment. No one looks forward to a painful experience, and although we consciously know the dental work is necessary, unconsciously we wish to avoid the pain. That desire sometimes takes over and we forget the appointment. Why would a man forget his wedding anniversary? Unconscious reasons? The excessive guilt feeling then is related to his concern that the lapse of memory will reveal his true feelings. People also forget because they are distracted, preoccupied, or the situation or occasion was not important enough. If one has excessive guilt about forgetting, it would be useful to try to understand what the meaning of the forgetting really might be.

Narcissistic Guilt

Another source of guilt is an action that results in a narcissistic injury leading to narcissistic guilt. Any act that makes us look bad or inadequate or is embarrassing or humiliating may produce guilt.

On the lighter side, there appears to be a massive effort to make people feel guilty and ashamed through the advertisements seen in the various media, particularly on television. Guilt-producing commercials such as those pointing out "ring around the collar," breath and body deodorants, ads pertaining to personal hygiene or appearance, including shampoos and skin conditioners, are often aimed at making you feel not only afraid that you will not be liked, but also that you will be disapproved of and shamed all because of your own neglect, a form of narcissistic guilt. Should you be ashamed and feel guilty if your wash is "tattletale gray"? A popular television program, "Soap," portrayed a housewife who spent most of her time cleaning her floors to remove "the waxy, yellow buildup," referring to a well-known commercial for a floor cleaner. It was an amusing caricature of the woman who is expected to be ashamed if her floor is not clean.

On a more subtle level but also appealing to a sense of shame are the cigarette ads suggesting that the man who smokes is a he-man, a virile cowboy with a tattoo. He usually gets the girl. The implication is that if you are not a smoker, you are a wimp. This is meant to make you feel inferior and ashamed if you don't smoke. Beer ads often take a similar tack.

The Need to Conform

A variation of narcissistic guilt is the need to conform. The failure to do so may produce guilt and humiliation. Although this is a desire particularly in adolescents who want to feel they belong and are one of the group, it may occur at all ages. The tenth-grader who does not have the right kind of leather jacket may choose to stay at home rather than risk the embarrassment of not looking the same as his classmates. Not conforming may lead to guilt in adults. A friend was invited to a wedding and wore a regular business suit. He was mortified to find he was the only one not in formal clothes. He felt ashamed and furious with himself because he had not checked on the dress requirements.

Fashion in women's clothing seems to be based on the need to conform. As the fashions change, many women feel ashamed if they are not wearing the latest style.

Religion

Religions have made important contributions to the establishment of a healthy conscience. Some formal religions, however, must be mentioned as great guilt producers as well. This may come not only from the dictates of the religion itself, but from the priests, ministers, rabbis, and parents who are the religious representatives. Some priests who are known to their parishioners as very strict and orthodox (strong guilt producers) are often avoided as confessors, and more lenient priests are sought. There is a special service in orthodox synagogues during the High Holy Fast Day of Yom Kippur in which men descended from a certain ancient tribe of Israel proceed to the front of the Temple and pray with their prayer shawls over their heads. A young Jewish boy was told by his religious father that if he looked up at these men, he would go blind. He could not resist looking and shortly thereafter was found to need glasses. He felt so guilty about having looked up that he was convinced it had affected his eyesight.

Accidents

Accidents can be guilt producers. This may range from serious auto accidents, in which the driver has injured someone or destroyed property, to accidental carelessness, such as an unintentional breaking of a friend's valuable vase. When the reaction is excessive guilt, even though the event was accidental, it is unhealthy guilt. A part of this is a reaction of rage against oneself for being careless and wishing that one had not caused the accident. The anger then generates guilt over the damage. Sometimes this is excessive. A woman told me that if she ever gets a spot on her dress, she must rush home and change, feeling guilty about her carelessness because everyone will think she is a slob. Many of the features of narcissistic guilt are related to feelings of being neglectful and careless.

There are numerous other guilt producers. It is important to evaluate each situation and be aware that no one can make you feel guilty if you don't accept it. *Just because someone says you are guilty does not make it so.* Too often the child in those of us with a strict conscience is quick to respond with guilt at any accusation. Don't jump to conclusions! The policeman behind us may be on his way home to dinner.

Guilt itself has survival value, and it is important for the continuity of society. Like so many other things, however, when it is excessive or leads to denial of other feelings, it can be harmful.

9

My Guiltiest
Moment

I decided to try an experiment. I asked a number of people what they remembered as their guiltiest moment, thinking that they would recall some incident in their childhood about which they might still have guilt feelings.

Many replied, "I am not going to tell you! That is one of my innermost secrets!"

Some were a little stronger. "Are you crazy? I am not going to tell you *that!*"

They were justified, of course. They were still feeling guilty and ashamed about the incident and could not reveal it. I then modified the question to ask, "What is the guiltiest moment you feel comfortable talking about?"

Here are a few of them:

My Own: When I was a little boy of 5 or 6, my mother became ill, and I remember feeling terrified, concerned that she might die. Our family doctor was like a god to us. Once we knew he was on the way (those were the days when doctors made house calls), we immediately began to feel better. He had been called and he arrived within the hour. He took her temperature, then handed me the thermometer, and asked me to wash it off. I carefully took it to the kitchen sink, but in the process of washing it, I dropped it and broke off the mercury tip. For a moment I stood staring at my shaking hands, which had betrayed me. I was terrified. I felt guilty that I had not lived up to his expectations of me. I was so ashamed, so helpless! At that moment I would have given my soul to make that thermometer whole again. I didn't know what to do. Finally, I managed to take the remaining stem of the thermometer to him, and I just handed it to him. He looked at it, glanced at me with a very knowing look as if to say, "I understand," and said nothing. I was enormously relieved but felt terribly guilty that I had damaged his thermometer. I can still feel the shame and guilt when I think of that incident and would gladly buy him a new one, a dozen new ones . . . even today.

Comment: I was terrified that my destructive act would lead to punishment and the loss of love of an idealized father figure. No comment on the symbolic significance of the thermometer, please! The guilt was overwhelming, despite his having clearly forgiven me. It was narcissistic guilt. I was ashamed and humiliated by the terrible thing I had done.

A 66-year-old woman: My guiltiest moment occurred when I was 8 or 9. All the youngsters in the neighborhood including myself had yo-yos. However, my yo-yo did not have the little metal ring for my finger as did all the others. I went into the ten-cent store, searched among the yo-yos until I found a loose ring, and took it home. My mother knew I did not have a metal ring for my yo-yo, because they cost 5 cents extra. When she saw it, she asked me where I got it. I said that I had found it in the dime store, lying loose among the others.
She inquired, "You *found* it?"
I murmured, "Yes!"
She said, "You march yourself right back downtown and return that ring, and you tell them what you did!" I dragged myself the two miles back to the store, envisioning all sorts of horrors, the least of which would be a lifetime in jail. The clerk received the ring indifferently and tossed it back into the pile of yo-yos. Still, I never felt so humiliated or guilty in all my life.

Comment: The aggressive act of stealing the metal ring led to mother's disapproval of her and the threat of punishment. Her rage at her mother for humiliating her and the fear of loss of her mother's love added to the guilt. Making her return the ring reinforced the narcissistic guilt resulting from the humiliation.

A 63-year-old man: When I was a youngster, we played golf at the club, and we had a caddy. At the end of the round of golf, we were handed a slip which I misread, thinking it said, "How was your game today?"

It actually said, "How was your caddy today?"

I wrote, "Horrible!"

Later I found out that the slip was to be an evaluation of the caddy. I felt guilty, believing that I might have caused him to lose his job. I quickly tried to retrieve the slip (which incidentally the caddy had already destroyed) and apologized to the caddy profusely for having misunderstood the request. I still feel guilty when I think about that incident, even though it was done in all innocence.

Comment: What appeared to be a hostile act had slipped out, revealing unconscious, unacceptable, hostile impulses leading to fear of loss of approval; he was overwhelmed with shame and embarrassment for what he had done.

A 54-year-old man: When I was in junior high school, I sat in the library next to a girl who got up to get a book from the shelves, leaving her purse on the table. I took the purse and left the library; but I felt so guilty all afternoon that I finally looked in her purse for her address, went to her house, said I had found the purse on the street, and returned it to her. I still feel guilty as I tell you this.

Comment: An act seeking gratification by the pleasure principle is revealed. It is unacceptable to his superego, and he is driven to return the stolen objects. His conscience is still not satisfied, and it continues to torment him.

A 30-year-old woman: When I was 13 years old, my mother became ill, and I was placed in charge of my 9-year-old sister and 3-year-old brother. While I was preoccupied with washing the dishes, I gave them money to go out and get ice cream from a truck that came by ringing its bell. As they went out, I cautioned them to be careful to look both ways before they went out into the street. The next thing I knew, I heard an awful scream and screeching of brakes. I ran out. My sister and brother had both been hit by a van that came up suddenly, which they had not noticed. They were not badly hurt, but I felt overwhelmed by guilt. I ran to tell my mother. She told me not to feel bad, that it was not my fault. No one thought I was guilty except me. But I still cringe when I think about it. I still can't forgive myself.

Comment: Her unconscious, unacceptable, hostile impulses toward her siblings (these are universal and ambivalent) were gratified by the accident. It was too close to her unconscious wishes, and she felt guilty about it, since the accident was an inadvertent result of her act. After all, she had sent them to the ice cream truck.

A 29-year-old woman: When I went to work in the secretarial pool, I met Charlie and we fell in love. We began living together and had a serious relationship. One day after we had been together for about two years, I decided to leave Charlie, having fallen in love with another man at work. I did it abruptly with little concern for Charlie. I didn't think it would matter much to him, but Charlie fell apart. He became seriously depressed, and I found out afterward that he had made an attempt at suicide. I have felt terrible since that time. I was overwhelmed with guilt because I felt I had wronged Charlie and should not have left him, even though he was not good for me. Charlie was a strange fellow, very moody, and he had his ups and downs. After two years, I felt very uncomfortable being with him, but I should not have left him that suddenly and my guilt feelings have persisted.

Comment: One might conclude that this was a story about guilt and sex. Although there may have been some guilt about that, the real guilt was over the hostile act toward Charlie. Her conscience was stirred up when she learned about Charlie's serious reaction to her leaving him, generating guilt in her.

A 39-year-old successful lawyer: When I was a little girl of 12 and my sister was 10, my mother had gone to great pains to make Easter outfits for us. She spent months cutting and sewing the dresses, and she even designed bonnets to go along with the outfits. When Easter Sunday came, my sister and I put on the dresses and bonnets, but we both thought they looked awful. We did not dare say anything to Mother about it, however; she had worked hard and was proud of her handiwork. We were sent off to church, but instead of going in, we walked around outside and avoided meeting anyone for fear they would laugh at us or think we looked silly in these outfits. I, being the older, felt I had influenced my sister to misbehave too. Ever since then, I have felt guilty for having betrayed Mother. I am too ashamed about the incident to tell Mother. She still does not know what we did.

Comment: A hostile act toward mother, revealing unconscious, unacceptable, negative feelings toward her. The superego reacts by developing guilt feelings that persist to today.

Zola Budd experienced in the Olympics what probably will be one of her guiltiest moments. Zola Budd was an 18-year-old South African woman who had established a fine reputation as a 1,000 meter runner and was selected to compete for Great Britain in the 1984 Olympics in Los Angeles. The match was particularly noteworthy because in this event the commentators had established that there were two people to watch: Zola Budd and Mary Decker, who represented the United States.

Zola Budd tells her own story (*Philadelphia Inquirer,* August 13, 1984):

> *We were around the curve and into the stretch. I was in front of Mary Decker and held the lead, feeling secure. Suddenly*

*from behind I felt a bump. I think it was Mary's knee on my
left leg. I was thrown off balance. I lurched a little and felt
pain as spikes raked down the back of my left heel. I fought
for balance; and suddenly I sensed Mary's falling, crashing to
the track.*

*I half turned and glimpsed her rolling toward the grass. I
couldn't believe it. It was terrible. I wanted to stop. I wanted
it all to end, and in truth, the race, for me, was really over.
I didn't know what happened except that Mary had somehow
run into me. At that point, I didn't think I had done anything
wrong. All I knew was that she had fallen from behind me,
but I did not think I had done anything wrong. Then I heard
the boos.*

*The booing came down like a tidal wave of concentrated
hostility. It was all aimed at me, and I realized that all of
these people were blaming me for Mary Decker's agony.*

*Finally it was over. I came in seventh. It hardly registered.
All I wanted to do was find out what had happened to Mary.
They had carried her from the track. I went back into the
entrance tunnel, and there she was. I walked straight over to
her and said the words that I wanted to get out the moment
it happened.*

"I'm sorry!" I said. "I'm sorry. I'm sorry."

*She looked at me, and she said, "Get out of here. Get out!
Just go. I won't talk to you!"*

*Despite everything that everyone had said to me, I now
thought that I was to blame. Mary Decker had been on TV in
tears saying exactly that—Zola Budd was to blame—and it
seemed so convincing.*

Comment: Regardless of what actually happened, in my
opinion, the unconscious impulse rising out of Zola's competitive
wish to win the race may have been gratified when she caused
Mary Decker to fall out of the contest purely by accident.
Apparently, Zola Budd felt no guilt at that point, being unaware
that she had had anything to do with Mary Decker's problem.
However, when the audience began booing, her conscience responded, and she was overwhelmed with guilt. Her own words tell

the rest of the story. Her conscience and her guilt could not be satisfied unless she was properly punished, and what more appropriate punishment than to lose the race they had both dreamed of winning.

A 43-year-old school teacher: When I was a freshman in college I went to the Bar Mitzvah of my young cousin who lived in a nearby town. I felt it was my duty to be there, and my parents expected me to attend. My rich uncle from Boston was there. He was the patriarch of the family and revered by all of us. He asked me how things were going at college. I said, "Fine, but I have an examination tomorrow." He looked horrified and asked me how I could be attending this party when I should be home studying for the examination. I was flooded with guilt and felt crushed. I took the exam and got an A. I called my uncle to tell him, and he said he couldn't understand how I could have gotten an A when I wasn't home studying. It still rankles me that he thought so little of my ability, and I continue to feel guilty about it.

Comment: She not only felt guilty for not living up to her uncle's expectations but also was furious with him for not understanding that she had gone to the party out of a sense of duty. She reveals the anger when she says, "It still rankles me."

It is significant to note that practically all of these guiltiest moments refer either to guilt feelings about hostile acts or narcissistic guilt. They illustrate the painfulness of a narcissistic injury. There were none directly related to sex, which could mean either that the people interviewed still felt too guilty about the act to tell it or that guilt about sex was not as strong as guilt over aggressive wishes.

The important finding is that often the guilt feelings persisted long after the incident. Even though the person may have been forgiven by others, the need of the individual's conscience to continue to seek punishment seems timeless and unlimited. These guilt feelings are still reversible, as we shall see in Chapter 10.

10

How to Deal with Unhealthy Guilt Feelings

It would be a mistake for you to begin with this chapter. This comment is not intended to make you feel guilty, but it is important to understand first where guilt comes from and why one has those guilt feelings in order to be able to deal with them effectively.

Learning to cope with guilt feelings does not mean eliminating them. This would not be useful and certainly not socially constructive. It is essential for everyone to have an appropriate amount of healthy guilt. If we believed that murder and rape were acceptable forms of behavior, we would all be in mortal danger.

It is the *overreactive guilt* with which this chapter deals. This is the unrealistic, tormenting, persistent guilt that is not beneficial and that continues to plague us, often despite our understanding that there is no reason to feel so much guilt. This excessive reaction is not only distressing, it can also be harmful.

There are no simple solutions to the complex problems of guilt. However, there are several steps that may lead to reasonable methods of handling guilt.

Recognition of the Guilt

First, one must be aware that anxieties, fears, depression, and emotionally based somatic symptoms may be due to unrecognized guilt.

Many people are not aware of having guilt feelings, but they may develop symptoms as a result of them. They have not accepted their own impulses, feel guilty about having them, and must deny them. The energy from these repressed wishes is then converted into fears or other emotional or physical disturbances.

All of us have feelings that are so powerful and frightening that we feel guilty for having them. The two main ones are powerful forbidden sexual desires and destructive, hostile, or angry feelings. There are others including jealousies, desires for power, and self-indulgences, to list a few.

Somerset Maugham's "Rain" has been referred to before because it is such a good example of this problem. The Reverend Davidson felt so guilty about his sexual feelings that he was driven to suicide when they were finally revealed.

Stella, the woman whose husband drank and stayed home all day, had numerous affairs and then felt guilty. She felt she should not have these sexual feelings, certainly should not act them out. Her problem was not her sexual feelings; they were normal. Her difficulty came from the denial of her frustrations and her anger at her husband. She sought some gratification for her need for love and sex in numerous unsatisfactory affairs.

What she had to do was accept her normal desire for love and affection and then deal with the *real* problem—her feelings about her husband. Having a number of brief sexual affairs did not solve her dilemma. In fact, her behavior added to her difficulties by generating guilt, which caused her great pain and suffering in addition to the anger and frustration at her husband, all of which she denied.

We have even more difficulty dealing with the guilt feelings generated by our angry or hateful impulses. All of us, at times, hate people whom we also really love. We may even, unconsciously, wish they would disappear or die. These feelings then generate guilt. We torment ourselves, believing we are cruel and horrible because we have such feelings. Sam's wife had developed Alzheimer's disease. He felt guilty about his resentment of her for being a burden. He repressed his feelings and began to have difficulty sleeping, developed high blood pressure, and became suicidal.

It is normal to have strong negative feelings toward people we love and are close to, but there are two aspects of this situation we must remember. The first is ambivalence. Ambivalence implies we can love and hate the same person and that *one emotion does not negate the other.* In other words, even though we may hate a parent, a spouse, or a child at the moment, it does not mean that the love for that person no longer exists. The reason we develop guilt feelings about our hostile impulses, particularly toward significant people in our lives, is that we assume it means that we do not love them. Ambivalent feelings toward our loved ones are universal.

The second important step in dealing with guilt about our angry, destructive feelings is a corollary to the first. We need to accept them, but this does not mean we must act them out. It is essential that we recognize that such feelings exist and that they may seem irrational, outrageous, and totally unacceptable. It is quite normal for a mother, after a long hard day, to wish that her children would disappear and that she would not have to deal with them again. If she will accept these feelings as normal, even though they seem unreasonable to her, she can avoid developing unhealthy guilt about them. She must remember that having feelings and acting them out are two separate things. It is all right to have the feelings; it is *not* all right to put them into action!

Gratifying these wishes directly is not the only way to deal with them satisfactorily. In fact, acting out our feelings is usually *not* the best solution. This is certainly true in the case of anger. A much more satisfactory answer is to utilize the energy constructively. If a young man is angry because his older brother is successful and he is jealous of him, the direct solution might seem to be to kill the brother. Obviously, this is no answer, although it has been tried many times since Cain and Abel. The jealous brother feels he has no right to be angry because of his brother's successes and tries to deny his rage. There are several ways he may proceed to deal with his anger. He may, for example, turn to drugs and alcohol, become a school dropout, or join a cult. A more satisfactory solution would be to recognize his anger, and although he may feel it is irrational, accept it as a human feeling. He can then use the energy thus released to achieve some success in his own life in a way that is socially acceptable and will bring him gratification. He should realize that he does not have to compete with his brother in order to be happy. He may finish school, go to work, and develop healthy social relationships.

Jealousy is a combination of insecurity and anger. It is another unacceptable emotion that is often denied because of guilt for having such a feeling. First, one must recognize and accept that such feelings exist. If they are excessive, the reasons for the jealousy need to be explored. One depressed patient I saw was unaware of his overwhelming jealousy of everyone who had more money than he did. It made him furious; he repressed the feelings and became depressed. With treatment, he was able to recognize that he felt insecure and believed that the solution to his insecurity was to have a million dollars. In truth, he was reasonably well off financially but was jealous of anyone who had more. He needed to work on the reasons for his feeling so insecure rather than being consumed by his jealousy of others.

Desires for power are present in most people. If they feel excessively guilty about having such feelings, they need to search within themselves for the reasons for the guilt. Perhaps they feel that if people knew they had such desires, they would be ridiculed or punished. Dread of disapproval by others is a powerful force, influencing not only our actions but also our emotions.

Overindulgences such as overeating, excessive drinking, and overspending may generate pathological guilt. First, one must determine if it is truly an overindulgence. It may be an excessively strict conscience that says any indulgence is too much. If it is, indeed, an overindulgence, belaboring the guilt will not solve the problem.

The excessive drinker who misbehaves at a party and spends the next day being contrite, seeking a variety of punishments to assuage his or her guilt feelings, would do better to use his or her energy to attempt to understand the basic problem. One must recognize the reason for the excessive drinking or overeating. If it is an effort to deal with an emotional problem, then that is the problem that must be resolved.

There are many other unacceptable feelings in all of us. The solution is not to torment oneself with overreactive guilt but rather to accept the existence of the wishes or desires, try to understand why we have them, and then to figure out ways of dealing with them realistically.

Review Our Standards

Once the guilt has been recognized and accepted, the next step toward alleviating unhealthy guilt is to look at the standards by which we measure our actions. If these standards are unrealistic, and we are trying to live in a perfectionistic, idealized way, we will find that we are tormenting ourselves with excessive guilt. We feel we are not attaining the ideals established for us by parents and other figures of authority, which we have accepted as the type of behavior that will please them. Failure to live up to these standards will make us feel ashamed of ourselves, a residue of the childish fear that mother and father will disapprove. It will generate guilt that can torment us and be truly harmful.

Of course, we should have high standards. As Robert Browning in his poem "Andrea Del Sarto" declared, "Ah, but a man's reach should exceed his grasp, or what's a heaven for?"

The important thing, however, is to try for realistic principles rather than unreasonable ones. The portion of our personality that is called the ego ideal needs to be modified if the standards are unreasonable or impossible. The whole subject of narcissistic guilt is related to the standards of the ego ideal. Joe felt he brought disgrace to his family by not making all *A*'s. That is unreasonable; no one can be perfect. Neither can one be totally dedicated to other people. We must recognize that *the ideal is that toward which we strive.* Although we should want to improve ourselves, we must be able to accept what we are able to achieve toward that end without feeling undue guilt and complete failure. We all have imperfections and limits. These limitations should be recognized and accepted. Once that is clear, we can modify our ego ideal so that we can live with it without developing painful amounts of guilt and feelings of humiliation or shame.

Forgiveness is an important factor in dealing with impossible standards. It means accepting ourselves as we really are. We must learn to forgive imperfections in ourselves. Phrases like "I will never forgive myself!" "I cannot forgive myself!" or "I will have to live with it the rest of my life!" suggest that the person feels the need for perpetual punishment because of his imperfect behavior. He suffers from self-hatred. He must, instead, explore the possibility of self-forgiveness in order to get on with his life and be useful to himself and others.

BLANCHE

Blanche was an attractive, intelligent 28-year-old woman who was determined to have a successful career in business. She had studied hard and received her M.B.A. from a prestigious school of business with high honors.

A year ago she had obtained a trainee position with a national bank and within nine months was an assistant manager who was authorized to grant loans up to $10,000 and approve checks to be cashed.

A man with whom Blanche had done business before asked to have a check cashed for $1,000. He had recently started his own business of installing swimming pools and needed the cash for his payroll. Blanche, satisfied that his credit was good, approved the transaction. The check bounced and the man disappeared.

Blanche was devastated. She reviewed the deal in her mind over and over. Why had she not been more careful? She had called the other bank on which the check was drawn and had been told that the funds were not there. When she confronted the man, he said the money was being transferred from another bank and, since this had occurred in the past, and he had been a valued customer of the bank for several years, she had trusted him. As a result of her guilt feelings, she was unable to sleep, lost weight, could not concentrate on her work, and became depressed.

When Blanche told her story she described a mixture of

reactions. At first she was terrified. She was certain that as soon as her supervisor found out what she had done, he would fire her and that would be the end of the career she wanted so much. She felt guilty for what she had done and dreaded the punishment. At the same time she described rage at the man who had duped her. She was able to admit that she even had thoughts of getting a gun and shooting the scoundrel. The anger was fanned by a deep feeling that he would not have done this to a man. Her fury, unfortunately, was quickly turned against herself and she became depressed.

When Blanche told her supervisor, he smiled and said, "You win some and you lose some. Learn from the experience." He then proceeded to tell her of a transaction in which the bank had lost $5,000 the week before.

Blanche, however, could not be consoled. She knew she could not take the transaction back nor make restitution for the error, although she considered repaying the loss personally. The debt continued to stare her in the face. She tormented herself with thoughts like "How could I have been so stupid? Why didn't I wait until the funds were in? Why was I so busy being a nice person to that customer instead of protecting the bank? Where were my brains?" Blanche was now suffering from narcissistic guilt, feeling she had done this to herself, and she continued to punish herself with her preoccupation, insomnia, and self-deprecation. Despite her supervisor's reassurances, she was unable to forgive herself.

Although Blanche's most serious problem was her narcissistic guilt, she had to explore all of her other feelings as well. She had to recognize and accept her rage at the customer and realize that she was turning that anger against herself.

As long as she could not forgive herself for the shame and humiliation she felt she had brought upon herself for making such an unforgivable error, she continued to be upset. She had hoped for a perfect record so that her career would advance rapidly and was furious with herself for having placed it in jeopardy. After a course of therapy she was finally able to accept her imperfection and realized that she was indeed doing a superior job. She was then able to turn her energies from punishing herself to doing even better work for the bank.

A sense of humor helps. Gordon W. Allport (1956) wrote: "The neurotic who learns to laugh at himself may be on the way to self-management, perhaps to cure." Similarly if individuals who feel excessively guilty can learn to laugh at themselves, they, too, would be on the way to controlling their feelings and being more comfortable with themselves. Lewis (1971) speaks of shame being dissipated with a touch of self-ridicule.

It is important to modify our ego ideal so that our standards are reasonable and attainable. It is helpful if we have a sense of our own value and strive to improve our self-image, even though as human beings we are by our very humanness imperfect. There is nothing wrong with looking in the mirror in the morning and saying, "I'm a pretty nice person!"

Examine Your Conscience

A third step to be taken in dealing with pathological guilt is to explore your conscience. Your conscience tells you whether you did the right or wrong thing, whereas our standards indicate whether or not we have achieved the goals of behavior we set for ourselves. Obviously, the two blend. The person who has a "guilty conscience" has a conscience that continues to tell him he did something wrong. One needs to look at one's conscience and determine whether or not it is unduly strict and generates excessive amounts of guilt. The conscience attempts to deal with our hidden wishes as well as our standards of behavior and is related to the superego, as previously described.

If we have cheated or harmed someone, we *should* feel guilty. A healthy conscience tells us we did wrong, we should regret it, and we should make restitution. Difficulties arise when we are unremittingly remorseful because our conscience plagues us, constantly telling us we did wrong, even if the act was a minor infraction for which we did try to make amends. It is not healthy to continue to worry continually and torment yourself without letup.

A very strict conscience insists that we live strictly by the letter of the law. Most of us, however, have some of the child in us that wants to do things just for our own pleasure. The man who takes a day off from work to go to a ball game, then feels so guilty about the terrible wrong he committed that he must tell the boss and resign from his job is overreacting. Most people probably shade the truth at some level. Many individuals who file a tax return and deduct an item that may be a doubtful deduction will be comfortable, fearing only an audit but not feeling guilty for having favored themselves. But the person who does this and then torments himself or herself, is unable to eat or sleep, and feels he or she has done something unforgivably wrong, is suffering from too strict a superego. That person must examine his or her conscience and modify it so that he or she can take some realistic action. When the superego is so strict that the guilt it generates is overwhelming, one usually ends up agonizing over it, a form of continuous self-punishment that is self-defeating.

An overly strict conscience leads to persistent feelings of guilt in cases that occurred many years ago when one may have done something that was wrong. It is important to accept the responsibility for that act and then be aware that the best solution to the problem is to *deal with the results in a constructive way.* Dwelling on the incident and continuing to be furious with oneself for having done that "unforgivable act" keeps the issue alive and does not allow one to solve it.

The woman who made a belittling remark to her friend and continues to torment herself about it years later has a pathological guilt reaction. The man who continued to be in a rage at himself for not having given up smoking had a right to be angry at himself and to feel guilty about having persisted with the smoking against his doctor's advice. He realized he had done wrong, but his rigid conscience would not desist. It is no longer productive at this point for him to continue to be furious with himself, torment himself with self-accusations, and become depressed. It adds to the physical difficulties resulting from the emphysema, which in a roundabout way satisfies his pathological need for punishment. Self-torture does not resolve guilt feelings!

A special situation where guilt was incapacitating was dealt with by the Israeli Defense Forces medical corps in developing a new treatment for shell-shocked soldiers. They were disabled by their experiences of battle, being required to do things unacceptable to their conscience such as shooting the enemy. The affected soldiers were treated by hypnosis at a military installation set up just behind the front lines. Under hypnosis, with the sound of gunfire in the background, the soldiers were enabled to deal with their guilt feelings and made to see that by doing what they had done, they were doing the right thing for their country, their families, and themselves, thus modifying their consciences. Most were able to return to their units within twenty-four hours. It must be said, however, that this is a very unusual, acute problem where hypnosis may have been effective in easing the soldier's conscience. In most cases, unfortunately, hypnosis has little effect.

Indeed, modifying the conscience is more easily said than done. Being aware that this is the problem can be a useful first step. Sometimes professional help is needed to try to modify the superego so that it allows us to live comfortably with ourselves.

Restitution

Step four calls for reasonable restitution. If one is guilty of having wronged someone, making sensible restitution can be helpful. Recompense has two components. It rights the wrong and acts as punishment by exacting something from you, material or emotional. You humble yourself when you apologize, accepting the blame and indicating regret; this painful action can help alleviate guilt. If you pay for a broken object and accept this as a genuine effort at restitution, it can ease the guilt. If the person who was wronged is unforgiving and persists in seeking additional punishment, the problem may be in the unrelenting person. A certain amount of anger is understandable in a person who feels he or she has been hurt, but an unreasonable, endless desire for revenge is not emotionally healthy and indicates a need in the person pursuing it. One should not accept guilt forever because the wronged person insists on it.

Guilty persons often seek punishment to relieve their guilt. Some religions use castigation to alleviate guilt. This relief may be obtained through additional prayers, fasting, or doing some charitable deeds. An extreme form of physical punishment such as self-flagellation has been used by some religious groups.

Making reasonable amends and being appropriately punished can be useful in relieving guilt. If the guilt persists in tormenting you, despite your efforts at restitution, you must search for other reasons for the guilt.

Those who have a low opinion of themselves will often blame themselves for an act they disapprove of and will generate excessive guilt, never forgiving themselves. All of us must develop a sense of our own value in order to grow up emotionally. If we feel inferior and inadequate, we will feel guilty if we have failed at a task, particularly if some authority figure says it is our fault. When the boss gives us a job to do and we are unable to complete it on time, we blame ourselves, feel guilt, and call ourselves a failure. Why doesn't the boss feel guilty for having given us too much to do? The employer does not see the task as a measure of his or her own worth so he or she has not failed, not to mention the fact that this person is the boss.

If we should feel guilty for loving ourselves too much, perhaps we should also feel guilty for not loving ourselves enough.

Emotionally mature individuals think well of themselves, feel they can deal with most problems that will arise, and do not feel excessively guilty if they have limitations. We all do. *Imperfection* does not mean *inadequacy*.

Excessive guilt feelings can be the result of overly strict parents who constantly blamed the child and made the child feel guilty for failing at a task. Children must be taught to accept responsibility; but if the method of teaching is excessive, either punitively or by undue shame and humiliation, the child may end up feeling he or she is unable to do anything right and may accept blame for everything that goes wrong, resulting in a constant feeling of guilt.

Summary

To summarize, if we do something wrong we should feel guilty. If, however, the guilt feelings persist and continue to torment us without letup, there are steps we can take to alleviate the suffering.

Five areas need to be explored and modified if one wants to deal effectively with excessive and unhealthy guilt.

First, we must *recognize* and accept guilt feelings if we have them.

Second, we should *review* and examine our unduly strict *standards of behavior* that generate excessive amounts of shame and embarrassment; the term narcissistic guilt has been suggested for this particular type of guilt, whether related to ourselves, our families, or other groups with which we identify.

Third, we must *examine our conscience* if we feel we have done something wrong. An overly strict, rigid conscience that makes us feel we have been bad, regardless of the judgment of the outside world, needs to be modified to conform to a more reasonable level.

The fourth step, *restitution,* is a useful means of alleviating guilt. Becoming a slave to a person we feel we have wronged is not proper restitution. It is excessive. Taking appropriate action to restore hurt feelings, payment for damages, and understanding how and why the wrong occurred is reasonable.

The last step calls for *self-forgiveness.* This does not mean constant, unreasonable self-exoneration. We must have healthy guilt and accept responsibility for a wrong, but if we blame ourselves for every wrong and never forgive ourselves, this is excessive. We must care enough about ourselves to accept our imperfections, strive to improve them, but still feel worthwhile.

There is no magic formula that will release us from all guilt, nor should there be. We must strive to function within the standards established by society's codes of acceptable behavior. Healthy guilt has survival value even in modern society. It is just as important today as it was in prehistoric days. When it is excessive, however, it no longer serves a healthy purpose and can make us ill. Sometimes we must consult professional help in order to recognize and understand the source of our problem and methods of coping with it.

Once we have made the appropriate modifications, we can utilize the energy we have been exerting to punish ourselves to do constructive things and live happier, more useful, and more satisfying lives.

Bibliography

Allport, G. W. (1956). *The Individual and His Religion*. New York: Macmillan, p. 92.

American Psychiatric Association. (1980). *Diagnostic and Statistical Manual of Mental Disorders*. 3rd ed.

Bailey, E. S. (1959). *Sexual Relations in Christian Thought*. New York: Harper.

Blum, H. (1983). Superego formation, adolescent transformation and the adult neurosis. Paper presented at the American Psychoanalytic Association, May.

Carter, J. C. (1907). *Law, Its Origin, Growth and Function*. New York: Putnam.

Chesney, M., and Rosenman, R. H. (1985). *Anger and Hostility in Cardiovascular and Behavioral Disorders*. New York: Hemisphere.

Edmunds, P. D. (1959). *Law and Civilization*. Washington, DC: Public Affairs Press.

Erickson, E. (1968). *Identity, Youth and Crisis*. New York: Norton.

Feldman, D. M. (1974). *Marital Relations, Birth Control and Abortion in Jewish Law*. New York: Schocken.

Fenichel, O. (1944). *The Psychoanalytic Theory of Neurosis*. New York: Norton, p. 244.

Foulks, E., Freeman, D., Kazlow, F., and Madow, L. (1977). The Italian evil eye: Mal occhio. *Journal of Operational Psychiatry* 8(2):28.

Frazer, J. (1947). *The Golden Bough*. New York: Macmillan, p. 204.

Freud, S. (1908). Civilized sexual morality and modern nervous illness. *Standard Edition* 9.

———— (1910). *Interpretation of Dreams. Standard Edition* 5.

———— (1911). Formulations on the two principles of mental functioning. *Standard Edition* 12.

———— (1914). *On Narcissism. Standard Edition* 14.

———— (1920). *Civilization and Its Discontents. Standard Edition* 25.

Friedman, M., and Rosenman, R. H. (1959). Association of specific overt behavior pattern with blood and cardiovascular findings. *Journal of the American Medical Association* 169:1286–1296.

Group for the Advancement of Psychiatry (1963). *Mental Retardation, A Family Crisis, The Therapeutic Role of the Physician.* Report No. 56, December.

Gaylin, W. (1985). *New York Times,* Science Section, p. 1, Feb. 5.

Huxley, T. H. (1898). *Evolution and Ethics,* Prolegomena. New York: Appleton.

Jackson, G. (1985). Interview. *People*, March 18.

Jenkins, R. L. (1950). *Feelings and Emotions.* Martin Reywert. Salem, NH: Ayre, p. 355.

Johnson, A. M., and Szurek, S. A. (1952). The Genesis of Antisocial Acting Out in Children and Adults. *PSA Quarterly* XXI.

Karpman, B. (1956). Criminal psychodynamics. *Journal of Criminal Law and Criminology* 47:9.

LaBarre, W. (1959). *The Human Animal.* Chicago: University of Chicago Press.

Lewis, H. (1971). *Shame and Guilt in Neurosis.* New York: International Universities Press.

Liebman, J. (1946). *Peace of Mind.* New York: Simon & Schuster.

Longman, P. (1984). "Everybody does it." *Philadelphia Magazine,* March.

Madow, L. (1972). *Anger—How to Recognize and Cope with It.* New York: Scribner.

———— (1982). *Love—How to Understand and Enjoy It.* New York: Scribner.

Meissner, W. W. (1984). *Psychoanalysis and Religious Experience.* New Haven: Yale University Press.

Noonan, J. T. (1965). *Contraception, A History of its Treatment by the Catholic Theologians and Canonists.* Cambridge: Belknap Press of Harvard University Press.

Piers, G., and Singer, M. (1953). *Shame and Guilt.* Springfield, IL: Charles C Thomas.

Plato. *The Republic, Book IX.* New York: Signet Classics.

Rangell, L. (1980). *The Mind of Watergate, an Exploration of the Compromise of Integrity.* New York: Norton.

Renshaw, D. C. (1982). *Incest, Understanding and Treatment.* Boston: Little, Brown.

Sheen, F. (1949). *Peace of Soul.* New York: Whittlesey House, p. 105.

Thomas, A., and Chess, S. (1977). *Temperament and Development.* New York: Brunner/Mazel.

Tuttman, S., Kaye, C., and Zimmerman, M., eds. (1981). *Object and Self—A Developmental Approach.* New York: International Universities Press.

Vital Statistics of U.S. (1982) Vol. 1.

Index

Index

Abortion, 59
Accidents, 136–137
Adolescence, 49–50
Aggressive instincts, 32, 67
Alcohol abuse, 120
Allport, G. W., 157
Anal guilt, 31
Anal morality, 31
Anger and guilt, 4, 67–80
    caused by church, 75–76
    fear of offending others,
      79–80
    illness-related, 76–77
    lack of guilt, 104
    manifestations of anger, 76
    narcissistic guilt, 91
    person-provoked guilt,
      71–74
    and psychosomatic illness,
      119
    turning anger inward, 77–78
    and unreasonable demands,
      71
Antisocial Personality Disorder,
    99–100
Authority figures, as guilt pro-
    ducers, 125–126

Bailey, D. S., 18
Blum, H., 31

Blushing, 91–92
Budd, Z., 145–147

Cheating, 100–101
Chesney, M., 119
Chess, S., 127
Child abuse, 34
Christianity, sex and, 18–20
Competitive drive, 14
Conformity, need for, 135
Conscience, 27–39
    anal morality, 31
    developmental timing,
      34–35
    Erickson's view, 29–30
    evolution of, 13–14, 20–21
    fear of punishment and, 35,
      37
    Freudian view, 28–29,
      30–36
    function of, 43
    impulse control in, 32–33,
      35
    incorporation of parental
      standards in, 33, 36
    internalized, 32, 36
    Klein's view, 28
    modification of, to deal
      with guilty, 158–160
    survival and, 13–14, 27

171